FIGURE IT OUT

A GUIDE TO WISDOM

Peter Megargee Brown

FOREWORD BY
ALEXANDRA STODDARD

THE LAWBOOK EXCHANGE, LTD.
Clark, New Jersey

Copyright © 2010 Peter Megargee Brown

ISBN-13: 978-1-61619-036-1 (cloth)
ISBN-13: 978-1-61619-037-8 (paperback)

THE LAWBOOK EXCHANGE, LTD.
33 Terminal Avenue
Clark, New Jersey 07066-1321

*Please see our website for a selection of our other publications
and fine facsimile reprints of classic works of legal history:*
www.lawbookexchange.com

Library of Congress Cataloging-in-Publication Data

Brown, Peter Megargee.
  Figure it out : a guide to wisdom / by Peter Megargee Brown ;
foreword by Alexandra Stoddard. -- Lawbook exchange ed.
      p. cm.
  Includes index.
  ISBN-13: 978-1-61619-036-1 (cloth : alk. paper)
  ISBN-10: 1-61619-036-1 (cloth : alk. paper)
  ISBN-13: 978-1-61619-037-8 (pbk. : alk. paper)
  ISBN-10: 1-61619-037-X (pbk. : alk. paper)
  1. Conduct of life. 2. Wisdom. I. Title.
  BJ1581.2.B718 2010
  170'.44--dc22
                                    2010003876

Printed in the United States of America on acid-free paper

To my beloved wife and partner,

Alexandra Stoddard,

my soul mate and muse,

who has given me over fifty-six years of love, affection,

and

the bliss of our companionship.

Grow old with me

The best is yet to be

The last of life

For which the first was made

Robert Browning

FOREWORD

Dr. Samuel Johnson understood that a writer has to turn over half a library to write a good book. This is certainly the case with *Figure It Out*. The wisdom that is central in twenty-seven categories has been distilled over fifty years of thinking, reading, and gathering experiences in all corners of the world.

Peter has always been interested in pithy gems of wisdom found in books, newspapers, magazines, and in conversations, and has the habit of saving them. He finds it a fun educational exercise to gather together and analyze what he determines is most valuable to know, to think about, contemplate, and to do. What started out as an informal daily exercise of collecting information and inspiration has evolved to become this rich reference guide to truth and wisdom. His concentration and focus on the best thinking available, collected over half a century, covering all aspects of his life, provides a fine and welcome perspective and vibrancy in this author's versatile life.

Peter believes that one of the most treasured things we have is time. *Figure It Out* is an effort to set forth a condensation, a honing in on the nuggets of gold, the keys of wisdom in just a few words. In a speech in England, His Holiness the Dalai Lama said that "many Americans like things quick, easy, and cheap," receiving roars of laughter. Dr. Johnson teaches that "the process is the reality." The pleasure for Peter has been in this stimulating, exciting process of observation and selection.

Because of his taking the time and making the effort to sift through thousands upon thousands of different bits of wisdom, the reader doesn't have to go through the same lengthy process, but can greatly benefit from this condensed intelligence. From this one person's collection of wisdom, readers reap the rich benefits of his acute mind as he burnishes his thoughts.

In order to write this book, Peter read hundreds of different authors, as a lawyer he tried hundreds of different lawsuits, and as an avid traveler with an insatiable curiosity he discovered the fascinating drama—and trauma—of the human lifetime. Aristotle teaches us that human beings desire to know. Because this one author has found such stimulation from the quest for truth in his love of learning, we, the readers, are the ones who inherit this wealth of knowledge that we all wish to acquire.

This valuable information will be useful to all of us who are seekers of wisdom and students of truth. Whether you are a reader, a writer, a historian, a philosopher, or a speaker at important events—even making a toast—this personal selection will delight you, uplift you, and help you to *Figure It Out*. In trying to determine what the most important areas of wisdom people should think and know about, he has identified the essential categories in our lives and filed all the research into file folders. Then he went through the material, reading everything over, and based on "good, better, best," he eliminated everything that wasn't good enough. This process of refinement goes on regularly. Peter came to believe the most important method of self-improvement is collating and inspecting words and phrases wherever you may find them.

Peter's training as a trial lawyer was to write briefs, and the judges would hurry him to "get to the point." In just a few words, a few paragraphs, to save other people's time, you have to aim at the center of the target. To be brief you have to chip away at the block of marble to come to the wise and wonderful truths that remain hidden to so many. His goal is to be concise and clear. Peter finds such delight in his learning process; he wants the reader to find his selection both attractive and fun. It takes a lot more work to write a short book, but the quality is greatly improved by what was cut out in the large round file under his desk...

Figure It Out is an honest simplification of his thinking. His love of words and their meaning shines throughout his book. You will discover that the thinking rings true, is both clear and honorable. He has eliminated the cute remarks, clichés, and the cynical, vulgar, or negative. These small capsules of intelligence help us to meet challenges and to know what's going on. Because the book is so succinct, the precise expression in a few words holds greater power. If something interests Peter and helps him, he believes it may interest and help others.

Life is far too complex not to have the proper tools to deal with various situations intelligently. When you read something that interests you, clip it out of the newspaper or magazine, or write it down. Peter and I acquired the habit of discussing our information and mutual knowledge. It's what we love to do on trains and planes, in airports, parks, or restaurants. We always have a pad and pen at hand to write it down, even at the kitchen table.

What makes a person wise is studying concentrated intelligence, derived from experience. Different situations require different resolutions. Common sense grows with experience. The more we actively participate in events and activities, the more we accumulate knowledge. By thinking through the meaning of the words—love, happiness, soul, philosophy, privacy, success, character, well-being, life, and heroes—we can seek a continuing education about the most important sensitivities of our lives. If we can gain more wisdom in our ability to love, to be happier, to be more trusting, we can appreciate the lifetime of curiosity and learning Peter shares with us. While it is true you can't become wise without experience, we can apply the basic elements of wisdom to try to learn more from whatever experiences we have, in order to become more skilled and knowledgeable. When we read, write, travel, seek beauty, listen to others as well as to music, strive to become more considerate, thoughtful, and appreciative, we will find, in the wide variety of our life experiences, that wisdom does seep through the cracks and light does appear.

I personally am grateful to Peter for this gem, a book of wisdom. Wherever we are, whatever we're doing, we're taking in these distilled bits of wisdom and inspiration to help illuminate our path. Basically, Peter goes back to the word and shows us how we build our intelligence, word by good word, thought by good thought. When we have acquired this life-affirming, life-transcending knowledge of timeless truths, the accumulated wisdom in our soul is not easily destroyed, nor is our happiness. Peter believes that collecting items of wisdom is a lifetime of satisfaction. His love of truth, beauty, and life itself is the unity that binds us together.

I am a witness that the author of *Figure It Out* is sharing with us, his family, friends, and readers, what a well-lived and loved life looks like close up. I intend to rely on Peter's invaluable guide all the days of my life.

Alexandra Stoddard

Stonington Village, Connecticut

Everything has been figured out
except how to live.

Jean-Paul Sartre

CONTENTS

L o E
V

No substitute is known to exceed the ecstasy and joy of love—a mysterious emotion that often enters our lives unexpectedly and with unexpected results—sweeping affection and feelings for another, accompanied by strong, sensual desire. We are most aware of the enormous power of love when separation intervenes in a cruel and heartless way. Paul's first letter to the Corinthians enlightened us all by his penetrating words: If I understood all mysteries but have not love, I am nothing. The key to all is love. It is the paramount gift of exchange.

The way to all is love
And ever has it been,
That love knows not its own depth
Until the hour of separation.

Khalil Gibran

Kindness expands love.

To be loved, be loveable.

Ovid

13

Recognize and appreciate immediately that something was accomplished well, that someone loved you too, that your day and night have been beautiful. Put these thoughts in your memory bank.

One can live magnificently in this world if, as Leo Tolstoy told us, one knows how to work and love.

From the first to the last Katherine [Mansfield]appeared to me a totally exquisite being. Everything she did or said had its own manifest vitality. I do not think it ever entered my head, at any time, to criticize her in any way. And certainly, for a long while I was secretly astonished that she should have chosen me.

John Middleton Murray

A sincere tribute to true love.

Is it so small a thing
To have enjoyed the sun,
To have lived light in the Spring,
To have loved, to have thought,
To have done?

Matthew Arnold

Wine is light held together with love.

Claire O'Classen, former nun

There is more self-love than love in jealousy.
François de La Rochefoucauld

To have love is to live with mystery.

I have mental joys
and mental health.
Mental wealth.
I've a wife that I love
and that loves me.
William Blake

Self-pity is the black hole of love.
Alexandra Stoddard
Self-pity signals incipient emotional decline.

Escape me?
Never—
Beloved!
While I am I, and you are you.
Robert Browning

The heart has its reasons which reason does not know.
Blaise Pascal

A person who loves himself has the advantage of having very few competitors.

A part of kindness consists in loving people more than they deserve.
                    Joseph Joubert

Intimacy is the greatest matchmaker.

Remember these three for all time: LOVE, TRUTH, and BEAUTY.

What the imagination seizes as Beauty must be truth.
                    John Keats

We live as we love by illusion, the essential stimulant to affection and the good life.

The most dangerous temptation is the temptation to prepare to live, instead of living. The future does not belong to you. Therefore, remember to live the best way you know now. The only perfection necessary is perfection in love, which can be reached only in the present. It's why we came into this world.
                    Leo Tolstoy

The greatest gifts of our genes to humanity are love, exuberance, and a passionate curiosity.
                    Kay Redfield Jamison

Love is light; light is love.

If You Want to Be Loved

Take what is given,

Respect it, exult in it, multiply it.

That is a law as old as man,

For then and only then

Shall you have anything

Worth giving back.

Study something; learn something,

Risk more than you think you can,

Care for something; become something:

If you wish to be loved.

> As told to Michael Drury in
> *Advice to a Young Wife from an Old
> Mistress*

It is not genius, or even love, that makes a person great, but kindness.

> Sam Pickering

More in love with desire than with the desired.

> Friedrich Nietzsche

I find as I grow older that I love those most whom I loved first.

> Thomas Jefferson

Rush is the nemesis of love.

Love is the whole story of a woman's life, it is but an episode in a man's.

> Germaine de Staël

Choose a job you love, and you will never have to work a day in your life.

> Confucius

It is a great thing when two souls are united to support each other in their work, in their successes and misfortunes, until the last silent minutes of the goodbye.

> George Eliot

There is a blessing in the air.

> William Wordsworth

It seems to me that our three basic needs, for food and security and love, are so mixed and mingled that we cannot straightly think of one without the others.

> M. F. K. Fisher

I believe you cannot kill love. Love is timeless, immortal.

> Alexandra Stoddard

Love provides a person with purpose in life. Intellect shows him the means to achieve that purpose.

> Leo Tolstoy

Love of Orchids

Sometimes a thin line separates healthy enthusiasm from pathological exuberance. One orchid grower started off with a single windowsill plant. Pretty soon he decided he wanted another orchid—first a red, then a pink, then a white one with spots. He couldn't stop, and now has a greenhouse with 200,000 plants.

One morning, his wife sat him down at the breakfast table. "Darling," she said, "you really must now decide whether you want to keep building your orchid collection, or have me with you here." Her husband replied, "That's the easiest decision I'll ever make. You're out of here, baby!"

Love and live
Live and love
Help ever,
Hurt never.
Love all
Serve all.

Sathya Sai Baba, Indian avatar

Riches and power are but gifts of blind fate, whereas one's goodness is the result of one's own merits.

Héloise, in *Love of Abélard* (c. 1164)—
second letter of many in their legendary
love affair

We have slept together,

Rose at an instant, learn'd,

play'd, eat together,

And wheresoe'er we went, like Juno's swans,

Still we went coupled and inseparable.

William Shakespeare

In *As You Like It*, the master creates for us the scene of true love

Be your own valentine.

HAPPINESS

Few should question today—despite our dire economic condition, well known and deplored—that we all, every one of us, will immediately choose the ultimate joy of happiness.

There is truth as well as understanding that while happiness is elusive, hard to define and difficult to maintain at a high pitch, still there is that satisfying enthusiasm, feeling the spark of contentment and love so necessary to achieve what we know as the good life.

You have to make your own magic!
> Alexandra Stoddard

Service to others is the first step to Happiness.

There is nothing in the world so much admired as a man who knows how to bear unhappiness with courage.
> Seneca

You cannot find happiness unless you first believe in it.

The happiest man is he who has no trace of malice in his soul.
Plato

For man comes to understand that the ethical life within society is a way to achieve genuine human happiness.
Jonathan Lear

She had that indefinable beauty that comes from happiness, enthusiasm, success—a beauty that is nothing more or less than a harmony of temperament and circumstances.
Gustave Flaubert, *Beauty of Madame Bovary* (1857)

We are often victims of our children's unhappy choices.

The greatest source of unhappiness is comparison.

On Fibber McGee and Molly, a radio program that began amusing Americans during the Great Depression, Molly used to say soothingly to her sometimes morose husband, "If it makes you happy to be unhappy, dear, then be unhappy."

Happiness is not automatic. It comes to us only with our own efforts and persistence. And sometimes happiness flies in to us like a bird.

Exercise for Your Enlightenment—
Write Down Your Own 10 Defining Words

Alexandra and Brooke Stoddard for several years have been defining themselves by their selection of ten words. This simple exercise has excited their spirit—and surprised them with its enlightenment! The exercise can be repeated later on with varied results…

Below I have composed my own ten defining words with the hope you will do so too.

Alexandra Stoddard wrote about this uplifting exercise in two of her recent books: *Feeling at Home* and *Happiness for Two*.

PMB Ten Defining Words

Gratitude

Remembrance

Kindness

Love

Beauty

Surfing

Generosity

Letters

Friends

Truth

Paradise is where I am.

Voltaire

America is more capable of enthusiasm than any other country.
Albert Einstein

The time to be happy is now,
The place to be happy is here,
The way to be happy
is to make others so.
Robert Green Ingersoll

Happy families are all alike; every unhappy family is unhappy in its own way.
Leo Tolstoy
These are the opening words of Tolstoy's famous novel Anna Karenina.

Truth and Beauty,
This is all.

The joy of your spirit is the indication of your strength.
Ralph Waldo Emerson

That is happiness; to be dissolved into something complete and great.
Willa Cather (1873-1947)
Inscribed on Willa Cather's gravestone in Jaffrey, New Hampshire

Pleasure is the beginning and the end of living happily.
> Epicurus (341-270 BC)

The reward of happiness is an active life lived with sweet reason.
> Aristotle

Every person seeks happiness. Our observation tells us so. And words of mentors: Plato, Hobbes, John Stuart Mill, Pascal, Winston Churchill, Learned Hand, Dwight Eisenhower, Eleanor McMillen Brown, Brooke Astor, John Marshall Harlan, J. Edward Lumbard, Alexandra Stoddard— and you!

I don't know what your destiny will be but one thing I know, the only ones among you who will be really happy are those who have sought and found how to serve.
> Albert Schweitzer

Seeking happiness outside of ourselves is like waiting for sunshine in a cave facing north.
> Tibetan saying

It is only by the constant cultivation of wisdom and compassion that we can really become the guardians and inheritors of happiness.
> Matthew Ricard

Apache Wedding Blessing for
Happiness for Two!

Now you will feel no rain, for each of you will be shelter for the
    other.
Now you will feel no cold, for each of you will be warmth for the
    other.
Now there is no loneliness for you;
Now you are two persons, but there is only one life before you;
Go now to your dwelling place to enter into the days of your
    togetherness,
And may your days be good, and long together.

Happiness is, after all, as mystical as it is elusive.

T R U S T

Marcus Aurelius, Emperor of Rome, was a good and noble person widely respected for his exemplary *Meditations* (now newly translated and introduced by Jacob Needleman and John P. Piazza). With exceptionally modest self-regard, Marcus devoted himself, among other kingly endeavors, to the practice of philosophy that, in turn, led his writings to be compiled posthumously in a classic book, *The Essential Marcus Aurelius*, praised as inspiring and useful, ready for emergencies, and a ready companion. The book does inspire us, offering an unsurpassed metaphysical vision, and the poetic genius of a worldly ruler whose realm comprised nearly half the peoples of the known world. His work has acquired a unique place among the writings of the world's great spiritual philosophers.

What is keenly significant about Marcus's writing is the author's insistence that *everyone trusted that he said what he thought and that he never did anything without good reason.* Never taken off guard or panicked, never hurried, hesitant, undecided or exhibiting a false kindness—nor on the other hand was he angry, irritable, or suspicious. Helpful and generous, forgiving and honest, he presented himself as one who could not be corrupted in the first place, rather than as a reformed man propped up by external assistance. Nobody would think that he was looking down upon them, but nor would they dare to think themselves superior to him.

As Marcus says, not easily will you find a person who is unhappy due to ignorance of what goes on in another person's soul, but those who do not follow the movements of their own soul will surely be unhappy.

If one sees death for what it is, and with the power of intelligence strips away all its imaginary characteristics, one will then understand death to be nothing more than a natural process, and it is childish to be afraid of a natural process. Moreover, this is not only a natural process, but is for the well-being of Nature herself.

What, then, could possibly guide us? Marcus asks. Only one thing: philosophy, and this consists in keeping the divine spirit within each of us free from...doing nothing aimlessly or falsely and with pretense, without need of another's doing or not doing something, and furthermore, accepting all that may happen and is allotted to us as coming from that source, whatever it is, from which we ourselves came.

Philosophy consists in accepting death with a contented mind, as nothing other than a liberation of those elements of which a living being is composed.

U.S President Ronald Reagan spoke succinctly with Gorbachev about the value of trust when he engaged in sensitive negotiations with officials of the Soviet Union bearing on the need for trust at all costs.

I did say something in our negotiations in Iceland in Russian: "*Dovorey no povorey.*" That means: "Trust, but verify."

Trust has, as long as memory itself, been the keystone to a good life of well-being and of confidence in other people whoever and wherever they may be. The daily newspapers today are filled with myriad examples of gross breaches of faith and startling scandals on all levels of society. Corruption is rank and crime of all kinds is rampant in many areas of the world. Without trust, healthy relationships falter and often die: morality, happiness, love, decency, honor, and good will are extinguished. To sincerely trust a person can enhance a trustworthy spirit.

To be a philosopher is not merely to have subtle thoughts, nor even to found a school, but so to love wisdom as to live according to its dictates, a life of simplicity, independence, magnanimity, and trust.

A sad and alarming financial situation has suddenly appeared on the horizon in the past decade: trust in financial markets has virtually evaporated, a major factor in causing the worst recession since the Great Depression in the 1930s. Two economic experts studying this serious problem, George Akerlof and Paul Romer, have served recently to hit the nail on the head: private investors, they say, have been shamelessly taking advantage of the United

States government by borrowing huge amounts of money, making enormous profits when times were good, and then "[leaving] the government holding the bag for their eventual—and predictable —losses."

These investors showed absolute disregard for fundamental principles of lending, failing to verify standard information about their borrowers, even failing to take care to ask for that information. "At a time like this, when trust in financial markets is so scant, it may be hard to imagine that looting will ever be a problem again, but the experts reviewing this bailout disgrace indicate that the looting of our government funds most likely will recur." In fact, these experts point out that an obscure incipient market called "credit derivatives" seems to be "taking shape as the next candidate for the looting of U.S. government funds."

We have been fairly and reasonably warned that some banks knowingly have placed bad bets while cynically counting on dipping outrageously into America's fragile treasury. This type of moral hazard, "when profits are privatized and losses are socialized, obviously played a role in creating the current mess."

Trust can rust and disappear.

The only way to make a man trustworthy is to trust him.

Henry Stimson

Henry Stimson—statesman, diplomat, lawyer, United States Attorney in New York City, author and outstanding leader in war and peace—displayed throughout his lifetime exceptional trust, character, and prescience. A model to emulate.

Never forget that a half truth is a whole lie.

> Fortune cookie

I had rather take my charge that some traitors will escape detection than spread abroad a spirit of general suspicion and distrust, which accepts rumor and gossip in place of undismayed and unintimidated inquiry.

> Judge Learned Hand

Love all, trust a few.

> Key advice from William Shakespeare's
> *Twelfth Night, or All's Well that Ends Well*,
> Act I.

L A W

Let no young man choosing the law for a calling for a moment yield to the popular belief [that lawyers are necessarily dishonest]—resolve to be honest at all events, and if in your judgment you cannot be an honest lawyer, resolve to be honest without being a lawyer. Choose some other occupation, rather than one in the choosing of which you do in advance consent to be a knave.

Abraham Lincoln

As a profession, lawyers do differ from other callings. This is not a fancy conceit, but a cherished tradition, the preservation of which is essential to the lawyer's reverence for his calling.

> United States Supreme Court Justice Lewis
> E. Powell, dissenting from the majority view
> in *Bates* v. *State Bar of Arizona* that the
> practice of law is a trade

The theme of my book, *Rascals: The Selling of the Legal Profession*, published in 1989, is that the American law profession should be largely free of crime, perfidy, greed, and sloth. Too many lawyers have tended to treat the practice of law as a trade solely for profit rather than as a profession for service to the public interest. As a result, essential elements of trust, honor, and confidence between client and attorney evaporate, leaving a rupture of litigation activity and resolution to the bar as a whole. As a result, the American law profession has suffered drastically.

In the 1980s I observed a turmoil among many law firms that left me stunned by "man's inhumanity to man," lawyers' perfidy in the face of greed, their shortsightedness, the evil that can pervade the good. Lawyers should set higher standards for themselves than the rest of society, because then, now, and in the future, lawyers literally act in the crevices of government, social, economic, and philosophic life in most civilized countries. If sufficient numbers of them are oblivious to such sensitive responsibilities, there is a reaction that affects us all.

Benjamin Cardozo, Chief Justice of the New York Court of Appeals, was brilliantly quoted in a pivotal lawsuit involving one of the major law firms in New York City that has formed the immediate basis for terminating outrageous behavior of numerous lawyers who had gone over the edge of honorable behavior. Here set forth are the words of Judge Cardozo that stirred the significant evolution of modern law practice, becoming an object lesson in the changing nature of law partnership—how so many first-class law firms became dollar-driven, with concepts of collegiality, honor, and trust dumped aside in the garbage can. He said:

Co-partners…owe to one another, while the
enterprise continues, the duty of the finest loyalty.
Many forms of conduct permissible in a workaday
world for those acting at arm's length are
forbidden to those bound by fiduciary ties. A
trustee is bound to something stricter than the
morals of the marketplace. Not honesty alone,
but a punctilio of an honor, the most sensitive, is
then the standard of behavior. As to this, there
has developed a tradition that is unbending and
inveterate…It will not be consciously lowered by
any judgment of this court.

In 1989 I was urged to publish *Rascals*, with the
encouragement of Chief Supreme Court Justice Warren E. Burger.
This was an appeal to restore honor and public responsibility to
the American law profession. I had personally observed the
profession's decline from the vantage point of senior partner and
head of the ethics committee in a large Wall Street law firm. I had
experience being an investigator and Counsel to the New York
State Crime Commission and Federal Prosecutor of Organized
Crime. I'd watched the once-honorable legal profession descend
to a bare trade, a bottom-line business.

My book reveals what some "leading lawyers" were doing to
the fabric of American society, the extraordinary rise of the "mega-
law firm," the sweeping corruption by licensed lawyers who knew

little or nothing of the profession's essential purpose and tradition.
In sum, too many lawyers are treating the practice of law as a
trade solely for profit rather than as a profession to benefit the
public interest.

Discourage litigation. Persuade your neighbors to compromise
whenever you can. Point out to them how the nominal winner is
often a real loser—in fees, expenses, and waste of time. As a
peacemaker the lawyer has a superior opportunity of being a good
man. There will still be business enough.
                        Abraham Lincoln

*There is a useless lawsuit in every useless word of a statute
and every loose, sloppy phrase plays the part of the typhoid
carrier.*

But where, some say, is the King of America? ... In America the
law is King.
                        Thomas Paine

*A young man begged Lincoln for advice. His reply was brief:
"Keep up with your correspondence."*

A sudden, bold, and unexpected question doth many times surprise
a man and lay him open.
                        Sir Francis Bacon

Justice Byron R. White on Taste and Style

In 1991 the Supreme Court upheld an Indiana public indecency law that banned nude dancing. Justice White wrote a dissenting opinion: "That the performances in the Kitty Kat Lounge may not be high art, to say the least, and may not appeal to the Court, is hardly an excuse for distorting and ignoring settled doctrine…in the words of Justice John Marshall Harlan, 'It is largely because governmental officials cannot make principled decisions in this area that the Constitution leaves matters of taste and style so largely to the individual.'"

The intention makes the crime.
Aristotle
This was good law 2500 years ago, and is today. Saint Thomas Aquinas considered Aristotle one of the greatest wise men. Pope Leo XIII pronounced him the only true philosopher.

Alfred Nobel, of Peace Prize fame, had a disregard for legal advice, creating his wealthy will by his own hand. He explained, "Lawyers have to make a living, and can only do so by inducing people to believe that a straight line is crooked."

Wherever law ends, tyranny begins.
John Locke

See The Art of Questioning: Thirty Maxims of Cross-Examination, *Peter Megargee Brown—original publisher Macmillan, The Lawbook Exchange, subsequent publisher. Currently available in a new edition with author's new prologue, in hard and softcover.*

Socrates at his own trial for treason boasted, unnecessarily, that he had a "diamonion," or guiding spirit—a private oracle—which immediately caused the 250 jurors to groan in disapproval...

As a consequence the jury convicted this icon and sentenced him summarily to death by drinking poison (in this case, hemlock). Subsequently, even the brilliantly balanced Aristotle was forced in exile in Turkey, where he died prematurely one year later.

The most useful, but least used, law is one not to be found on the statute books—the *Law of Unintended Consequences*, . . . formulated by an astute observer of the human condition, who noted the frequency with which governmental remedies inflict more harm than the ills they are intended to cure.

Honorable James Lane Buckley,
Yale Class of 1944

The law is a sort of hocus pocus science.

Charles Macklin

Exchange in the 1878 trial of artist James McNeill Whistler's libel suit against critic John Ruskin, who had criticized Whistler's painting *Nocturne in Black and Gold*: I have seen, and heard, much of Cockney impudence before now, but never expected to hear a coxcomb, a conceited fop, ask two hundred guineas for flinging a pot of paint in the public's face. **Cross-examiner for Ruskin, sarcastically:** The labor of two days, then, is that for which you ask two hundred guineas? **Whistler's reply:** No, I ask it for the knowledge of a lifetime.

We may affirm absolutely that nothing great in the world has been accomplished without passion.

> Hegel

The law is a jealous mistress, and requires a long and constant courtship. It is not to be won by trifling favors, but by lavish homage.

> United States Supreme Court Justice
> Joseph Story

Freedom of expression is the matrix, the indispensable condition, of nearly every other form of freedom.

> Justice Benjamin Nathan Cardozo

Scientist William James understood that philosophy and psychology were not just technical matters but more the meaning of life itself. With this perspective we can see and feel the divine energy and spirit of the cosmos.

The Legal Mind at Work??

Judges lie, then lawyers lie, then clients lie.

> Alan M. Dershowitz, Esq., 1993

Lawyers don't lie.

> Alan M. Dershowitz, *in a contradictory*
> *interview with Casper Citron on WOR*
> *radio, NYC, December 10, 1994*

The life of the law has not been logic: it has been experience.

> Justice Oliver Wendell Holmes, Jr.

A wise and experienced trial lawyer knows the whole lawsuit—top to bottom—both sides of the case, including the idiosyncrasies of the judge.

Pardon one offense, and you encourage the commission of many.

> Pubilius Syrus

He who only knows his own side of the case, knows little of that.

> John Stuart Mill

Let us never negotiate out of fear, but let us never fear to negotiate.

> John F. Kennedy

Truth cannot die with time and with the change of generation.

> His Holiness the Dalai Lama

Franz Kafka's *The Trial* (1925) is the surreal story of Joseph K., a man who is accused of nameless charges that can never be fully refuted and about which he can get no firm information. The Clinton White House seems to have drawn on this 1925 trial parallel— see comparison below:

The Trial (1925)	Whitewater Scandal, March 7, 1994
"K. went on, 'Though I am accused of something, I cannot recall the slightest offense that might be charged against me.'"	"No one has accused me of any abuse of authority in office…There is no credible evidence and no credible charge that I violated any criminal or civil federal law." –Bill Clinton, March 7, 1994
"K. went on, ' There can be no doubt that…behind my arrest and today's interrogation, there is a great organization at work.'"	"[The Whitewater controversy] is a well-organized and well-financed attempt to undermine my husband, and by extension, myself." –Hillary Clinton, in the May 1994 issue of *Elle* magazine
"K. is told, 'One must really leave the lawyers to do their work, instead of interfering with them.'"	"Why don't you guys let the special counsel do his job?" –Bill Clinton, to members of the press, March 21, 1994

The spirit of liberty is the spirit which is not too sure that it is right.
Judge Learned Hand

I shall never ask, never refuse, nor ever resign an office.
Benjamin Franklin

The power of choosing good and evil is within the reach of all.
Unknown Origin

It is hard to catch the thief if he is a member of the family.
Arabic saying

When Winston Churchill died he had already planned the details of his funeral and his distinguished burial under the floor of Westminster Abbey. On its surface were set forth these two succinct words:

REMEMBER CHURCHILL

D E A T H

We live and die
But which is best
You know more than I.

Lord Byron, *Don Juan, VIII*, 1823

Live as if you were to die tomorrow, but learn as if you will live forever.

Mahatma Gandhi

I find it stunning to be told, with some conviction, that in our world today we can be certain that every single one of us has a "common ancestor!"

My father, George Estabrook Brown, wished to stun us further by his insistence to our family (a brother, George, and two sisters, Harriet and Barbara) that my father revealed to us *his own family motto* went back to an ancient crest in Holland engraved with these succinct three words:

LEARN TO DIE

This bit of wisdom came to our family set in the French language (*"apprendre à mourir"*). Candidly, my father, a disappointed stock broker and genealogist, was more than particularly fond of this family coat of arms and crest, determined to live by the words, and sought to teach his children to do the same. He wore a gold ring on his left small finger (engraved by Tiffany) with these three words adjacent to the sacred family crest of a handsome eagle in flight. My brother George coveted my father's gold ring as well as the inscription in French—"learn to die."

All went well until I fell in love with Alexandra Stoddard in 1973 and discovered, while she liked the ring, she was somehow disappointed in the inscription on the ring itself, *"apprendre à mourir."* She gently but firmly asked me to please amend the words on the ring to *"apprendre à amour"*—"learn to *love*." I told Alexandra that I would be happy to have Tiffany amend the words to her liking, which I enjoyed as well: "Love, not death!" I exclaimed.

There was only one problem: my brother, George, was offended by what he called the indignity of changing the family crest ring in this fashion. I tried not to be involved in this quarrel about nothing of any importance to me, at least as far as I could discern. *Who cared? George* got the ring! *Didn't he?*

Our family quickly became interested in this curious dispute about death and love; I felt that this was a philosophical argument that was best terminated by facing it calmly without irrational anxiety. I made the mistake of suggesting to George that the thing he

should be philosophical about was death itself. I recounted awk-
wardly the last day of Socrates, who spoke to his friends gathered around him as he serenely drank the fatal cup of hemlock.
Death, he mused to them, "might be annihilation, in which case, it
is like a long dreamless sleep or maybe a flight of the soul from
one place to another…" Death had nothing to be feared, he said.
Cicero himself added that to philosophize is to "learn how to die."
For me, that settled the matter!

Old Man and His Dreams

"I picked up an old man," author Malachy McCourt tells
us, "driving in a hard, driving rain. When he got out he said:
'Thank you, sir, *may you have a happy death.*' He smiles.
When you think about it, a happy death means that you have
had a happy life. And I think I have. These days the simple things
are appealing…

Diana, our closeness and love. The grandchildren…I've
learned acceptance and letting go and keep a sense of humor
about this absurd condition. I'm having my dream one at a time."

*Ralph Waldo Emerson, on his deathbed, was visited by the
local priest: "Mr. Emerson," he said, "have you reconciled
yourself with God?" Emerson opened one eye, and replied,
slowly: "I did not know we had ever quarreled."*

*Remember the poet Virgil, who cautioned us that it is easy to
descend into hell but difficult to return.*

I am ready to meet my maker. Whether my maker is prepared for the ordeal of meeting me is another matter.

Winston Churchill

Live each day in the loving energy of eternity, while also feeling each day you're living on borrowed time.

Alexandra Stoddard

Vital statistic (2008): Smoking causes one in five deaths in the United States.

Our Ongoing Debate about God and Death

The web site BlasphemyChallenge.com has brought forth over 400 young people in a campaign in 2006 to deny the existence of God. Journalist Jerry Adler, on the other hand, tells us this is the ultimate no-win wager: "As the 17th-century French mathematician Blaise Pascal calculated, it can't be settled until you're dead, and if you lose, you go to hell."

Seneca gave good advice on how to react as death approaches: to reserve for yourself only the remnant of life, and set apart for wisdom only that time which cannot be devoted to any business. How late it is to begin to live just when we must cease to live! We must get started now, while we are healthy in body and mind.

When I go from here, I want to leave behind me the world richer for the experience of me.

Brooke Astor

A bronze memorial honoring Robert Louis Stevenson can be found at Saint Giles Cathedral in Edinburgh, Scotland. He was a superb writer, author and philosopher, long suffering from tuberculosis. His last words were: "Death is so final."

The desire for death shortens life.

There is a ripeness of time for death...when it is reasonable we should drop off, and make room for another growth. When we have lived our generation out, we should not wish to encroach on another.

Thomas Jefferson

When you, at the end of your life, proceed through the Main Gate, you go alone—remember without your guru.

Mark how fleeting and paltry is the estate of MAN—yesterday in embryo, tomorrow a mummy or ashes. So for the hairsbreadth of time assigned us, live rationally, and part with life cheerfully, as drops the ripe olive, extolling the season that bore it and the tree that matured it.

Marcus Aurelius

It is impossible that anything so natural, so necessary, and so universal as death should ever have been designed by Providence as an evil to mankind.

Jonathan Swift

So-called "retirement," much anticipated by millions, is more often a sad and dangerous descent in life. Instead, keep engaged with living every day that remains, cultivating joy with loved ones until the end.

When a man dies, if he can pass enthusiasm along to his children, he has left them an estate of incalculable value.

Thomas Edison

The soul, possessing elevation of thought and the contemplation of time and being, will not view death as something to be feared.

Plato

It is as natural to die as to be born.

Sir Francis Bacon

The endless debate about the existence of God makes me appreciative of the sage conclusion of Goethe: "Believe, Sir, you have nothing to lose."

The idea is to die young as late as possible.

Ashley Montagu

Our souls survive this death.
>   Ovid

The longest journey is the journey inwards of him who has chosen destiny.
>   Dag Hammarskjöld

"*In the long run*" is a misleading guide to current affairs. In the long run we are all dead.
>   John Maynard Keynes

It is not death, but dying which is terrible.
>   Henry Fielding

It is better to live rich, than to die rich.
>   Samuel Johnson

Death is nothing to us.
Since when we are,
Death has not come.
And when death has come,
We are not.
>   Epicurus

Death confounds us with its timing and its apparent disregard of human plans and hopes.
>   Thomas Moore

More young people die of behavioral misadventures than of all diseases combined.

> Lewis Lipsitt

Death keeps no calendar.

> George Herbert

Be ashamed to die until you have won some victory for humanity.

> Horace Mann

Man does not move in cycles, though nature does. Man's course is like that of an arrow.

> S. T. Coleridge

Old and young, we are all on our last cruise.

> Robert Louis Stevenson

Few artists have exhibited the brilliant flair for color of Henri Matisse—even at the end of his life, in bed, making superb cutouts.

It requires more courage to suffer than to die.

> Napoleon I

The mere thought of death somehow makes every blessing vivid, every happiness more luminous and intense.

> Tony Snow

The great primordial plot: birth, love death.

> Carol Shields, novelist, Pulitzer Prize winner

Novelists would despair and possibly go broke if they were denied using the age-old themes of birth, love and death.

It is not death that a man should fear, he should fear never beginning to live.

> Marcus Aurelius

Alexandra, I will die when my usefulness is up.

> Eleanor McMillen Brown

Alexandra's mentor was an exceptional artist of interior design in the Edith Wharton tradition. Her inventor father gave her good advice and a fund to start her own business. She worked hard, loyally and persistently. She never faltered and will be remembered for all time for her decency, her exceptional honor and discipline. She died five days shy of her 101st birthday.

Last Words

I'm still alive.

> Daniel Webster (1782-1852)

S O U L

Any mention of "soul" can cause, in most areas of our lives, both comfort and discomfort, simultaneously. The reason may be that somehow no one seems to know for sure exactly what the definition of the soul means. We do nonetheless experience a sense of uplift, a gracious feeling that inspires us and, in critical times, lends us a spirit of hope, perhaps a stirring of aspiration and a touching encounter with beauty, elements of truth, virtue, as well as a visit to the good life.

Socrates, despite his innate evasiveness to answer a question, instead, spent his precious time annoying fellow Greeks with questions that served to undermine and disturb them, chastising each of them repeatedly until they would become undone. This insipid habit eventually led to his indictment by over 200 senior colleagues on ambiguous, trumped up charges of impiety, as well as misguiding the callow youth of Athens. Socrates was condemned by over 200 and sentenced, after a weak if arrogant defense, to die with several swigs of hemlock poison. He died surrounded by curious citizens who may have felt maligned by Socrates's criticism that they were caring too little about truth and wisdom and the greatest improvement of their soul.

Are you ashamed of heaping up the greatest amount of money, and caring so little about the wisdom and truth and the greatest improvement of the soul?

> Socrates, 339 B.C., while annoying his
> constituency

What does the word "soul" mean… no one readily can give a satisfying definition of the soul. But we know what it *feels* like. The soul is the sense of something higher than ourselves, something that stirs in us thoughts, hopes, and aspiration which go out to the world of goodness, truth, and beauty. The soul is a burning desire to breathe in this world of light and never to lose it—to remain children of light.

> Albert Schweitzer

Acquire the kind of wealth which cannot be stolen from you, which people in power cannot take from you, that will stay with you even after your death, never diminishing and never disappearing. This precious wealth is invisible. It is your own soul.

> Indian proverb

Joking is undignified; that is why it is so good for one's soul.

> G. K. Chesterton

Our soul is the sign of eternity.

> William Ellery Channing

The will to do, the soul to dare.

> Sir Walter Scott

Thomas Paine had the knack to arouse the militant spirit with artful, well-chosen words: These are the times that try men's souls. The summer soldier and the sunshine patriot will, in this crisis, shrink from service of his country, but he that stands by it now, deserves the love and thanks of man and woman. Tyranny, like hell, is not easily conquered, yet we have this consolation with us, that the harder the conflict, the more glorious the triumph. (*The American Crisis of December 1776*)

"Spirit-energy"* is surely the life force propelling us forward to the good life.

> * Coined by Alexandra Stoddard

I call spirit that part of man which has independent existence and gives us the understanding of life.

> Marcus Aurelius

Virtue is a kind of health, beauty and good habit of the soul.

> Plato

Art is an exquisite expression of the soul.

For what shall it profiteth a man that he gain the whole world and loseth his soul?

> Saint Mark

The nature of a soul is so mysterious that no matter how hard you try to understand it, we will never be able to define it.

> Heraclitus

It is the marriage of the soul with nature that makes intellect fruitful, and gives birth to imagination.

> Henry David Thoreau

The upright stance and the development of speech…are some of the attributes of man that have raised him above the animal kingdom. This structure is responsible for his conscience, his morals, his ethics, his religion, nature, and his aesthetics. It is the source of all his spiritual aspirations and endeavors.

> A. A. Mason, psychoanalyst

We must have richness of soul.

> Antiphanes, 331 B.C.

Hatred is the winter of the heart.

> Victor Hugo

The spark of the spirit ignites at birth and continues eternally as your soul.

TIME

This small piece is written February 4th, 2009 to celebrate, by concentration on the significance of time. What is it? What does time mean to us—today, tomorrow, yesterday?

The more we think about our time on earth, the more we dwell on the passion of the few moments left to us...

The statisticians—bless them—come up with excruciating wisdom by cited numbers, so fiercely concrete to cause our deep thought of our own spare time left here, to be alive, passionately aware of the joys and happiness of the past and the present, and in contemplation of the future.

How long do we live? I was told a few days ago that our average lifespan is 25,550 days. That revelation starts our mind whirling... We wonder whether we have been wasteful, careless, thoughtless about myriad things, neglectful of loved ones, mindless of our friends and neighbors, oblivious of those in poverty, illness, distress in a period of overwhelming financial crisis similar to the Great Depression (1929-1945). A dreadful time, as my father would try to explain to me in our library at 1172 Park Avenue 79 years ago: The economics of the situation were not quite clear—nor are they, frankly, today… Still time is our dearest treasure. The present is the diamond of time. No lost time is retrievable.

I do not regret that my time (borrowed time) is running out. Again the statistician has advised me a week ago that the average person lives a lifespan of only two billion seconds. Reluctantly, I'll be leaving soon and will not be back again.

Love to all, especially my beloved Alexandra

Sincerely, Peter

You may ask me for anything you like except time. Work is the scythe of time.

Napoleon

Napoleon was on board a ship to his second exile—again a remote spot, in August 1815. He mused about writing his memoirs…(the work?)

We learn only when it is too late that the marvel is the passing moment.

François Mitterand

The times are out of joint when madmen lead the blind.

William Shakespeare, *King Lear*

Do not wait for life. Do not long for it. Be aware, always and at every moment, that the miracle is in the here and now.

Marcel Proust

Affliction is the good man's shining time.

Edward Young

This English poet, as quoted by Abigail Adams, refers to General Washington's timely attack on Trenton in December 1776.

We all find time to do what we really want to do.

William Feather

The butterfly counts not months but moments; and has time enough.

Rabindranath Tagore

Time present and time past
Are both perhaps present in time future,
And time future contained
In time past.

T. S. Eliot

Lost time is never found again.

Benjamin Franklin

We shall never have more time. We have, and have always had, all the time there is. No object is served in waiting until next week or even until tomorrow. Keep going… Concentrate on something useful.

Arnold Bennett

Song of Solomon

Winter is past,
Snow is over and gone:
Flowers appear on earth;
The time of the singing of birds is come.
And the end of all our exploring
Will be to arrive where we started
And know the place for the first time.

T. S. Eliot, Little Gidding, *Four Quartets*

Time is the wisest counselor of all.

Pericles

After spending considerable time on Andrew Marvell and Robert Herrick in the class I taught on 17th century British poetry, I felt I'd exhausted the concept of *carpe diem*, or seize the day. I was surprised, however, by one student's answer to the essay portion of the mid-term exam. He had given a vivid account of Marvell's rising from bed, opening the curtains and viewing the sunrise. I was confused about what this had to do with *carpe diem* until I read the last line of his answer: . . . "and this is how Marvell sees the day."

Contributed by Jeanne A. Barnes

The first thing you learn in marriage is that you are not in charge of your own time.

Brooke Stoddard

Imagination is the morning; memory is the evening of the mind.

Ralph Waldo Emerson

How moments fly when we're immersed in the swing of what we like to do.

Tomorrow's life is too late. Live today.

Longinus (1ˢᵗ century AD)

Time leaks away; we must use it wisely since we cannot bank it.

Herbert Brownell and General Lucius Clay were instrumental, after extraordinary efforts, in trying to persuade Dwight Eisenhower to run for President in 1952. Eisenhower continued to be painfully noncommittal, confounding friends and foes alike. The time for the Republican convention neared, with Robert Taft on the verge of sewing up a majority of delegates.

Finally General Clay, the closest confidant of Eisenhower, could stand it no longer. Time was running out. Further delay would be fatal. When the moment for decision finally arrived, Clay moved in to tell Eisenhower:

"Goddamn it, Ike, it's time to do this. It's time to decide or it will be too late."

Herbert Brownell, *Advising Ike*

Every human being has exactly the same number of hours and minutes every day . . . you can't save time to spend it on another day.

> Denis Waitely

Procrastination is the thief of time.

> Edward Young

It is a mistake to look too far ahead. Only one link in the chain of destiny can be handled at a time.

> Winston Churchill

Time is the least thing we have.

> Lillian Ross

You are in charge of your own time, which is the difference between freedom to live well or slavery. Maybe better to appoint a divine soul to be your Guardian of Your Time on Earth, just as author Alexandra Stoddard is my own treasured guardian of my time on Earth.

Darwin was perhaps more than a wily realist, with an inclination toward objective truth and pragmatism. He stubbornly, sometimes gently, insisted that while life over time "tends to progress," yet the future of that progress, like the past, will continue as "a vast stretch of geologic time, unstructured by plan or purpose, beyond our immediate control or imagination."

Let anyone try, I will not say to arrest, but to notice or attend to, the present moment of time. One of the most baffling experiences occurs: where is it, this present? It has melted in our grasp, fled before we could touch it, gone in the instant of becoming.

William James

Time, for all, moves constantly in one dimension—forward. For young and old nothing can redeem time lost or wasted. Time is our greatest gift. Try to move the hands of a clock backwards...

In our daily life and business we can discover contentment as well as economy by observing Brown's Law: The time necessary to complete a task or obligation will take considerably longer than you think it will.

Time is the most valuable thing a man can spend.

Theophrastus

Time is the best teacher, if it encompasses experience.

Delay rots our desire for success and withers our ambition.

Lost, yesterday, somewhere between sunrise and sunset, two golden hours, each set with sixty diamond minutes. No reward is offered, for they are gone forever.

Horace Mann

Nine tenths of wisdom consists in being wise in time.
Theodore Roosevelt

The trouble is that you think you have time.
Buddha

Time is the devourer of all things. (*Tempus edax rerum*)
Ovid

The past, the present and the future are really one: they are today.
Harriet Beecher Stowe

When we wonder about the intricate precision of the calendars of the ancient Mayans, we know they regarded time as precious.

There is only one time when it is essential to awaken. That time is now.
Buddha

Chronobiologists (scientists who study the effects of time on life processes) argued recently we should all be thankful that evidence has just been revealed that, for those who imbibe alcohol, the liver best detoxifies booze between five and six PM.
Jennifer Acherman, *Ideal Time for a Drink*
No wonder this period is called the happy hour.

If you take care of each moment, you will take care of all time.

Buddha

Make use of time, let not advantage slip.

William Shakespeare

Punctuality rises to virtue in today's tardy world.

I'm a pessimist about tomorrow, but I'm an optimist about the day after tomorrow.

Eric Sevareid

Eric Sevareid, a brilliant journalist, wrote about pessimism and optimism—often quoted for its comforting words.

If the present criticizes the past, there is not much hope for the future.

Winston Churchill

You will never "find" time for anything. If you want time you must make it.

Charles Buxton

With the past, I have nothing to do, nor with the future. I live now.

Ralph Waldo Emerson

It is not that we have so little time, but that we waste so much of it.

Seneca

Time eases all things.

> Sophocles

And if not now, when?

> The Talmud

Guard well your spare moments. They are like diamonds. Discard them and their value will never be known. Improve them and they will become the brightest gems in a useful life.

> Ralph Waldo Emerson

The past does not exist. The future has not begun. The present is an infinitely small point in time where the nonexistent past meets the imminent future. At this point—which is timeless—a person's real life exists.

> The Talmud

Sometimes I wake up in the morning and there's nothing doing, so I decide to *make something happen by lunch.*

> Irving (Swifty) Lazar

This Roman emperor was a remarkably balanced philosopher: How much time he gains who does not look to see what his neighbor says or does or thinks, but only what he does himself, to make it just and holy.

> Marcus Aurelius

Time carries all things, even our wits, away.
> Virgil

Take time every day to sit quietly and listen.
> Buddha

—here, now, always.
> T. S. Eliot

Unfortunately, waiting is a national occupation, utterly unproductive and bitterly boring. In the Broadway play "Waiting for Lefty" the poor single character never left the stage.

Do not bother about what will happen someday, somewhere, in the faraway distance, in the future time; think and be very attentive to what happens now, here, in this place.
> John Ruskin

Plato said we can't live counterclockwise.

The past is history
The future is a mystery
This moment is our gift.

Light tomorrow with today.
> Elizabeth Barrett Browning

The hurrier I go, the behinder I get…
> Swedish proverb

Splendor in the Grass

Though nothing can bring back the hour

Of splendor in the grass,

Of glory in the flower,

We will grieve not,

Rather find

Strength in what remains behind…
> William Wordsworth

Misspending a man's time is a kind of self-homicide.
> George Savile, Marquess of Halifax

READING

The National Endowment for the Arts found that 53 percent of Americans had not read a book in the previous year! Yet in the year 2007, 400,000 books were published in the United States. And seven percent of adults polled (or fifteen million people) did creative writing, mostly for personal fulfillment.

Rachel Donadio reports in the *New York Times* that as people grow older, they have more time and more money—and something to say...Fewer people may be reading books but, on the other hand, more are publishing their own. In the early 1980s I founded a small publisher, Benchmark Press, a most helpful, encouraging support for the half dozen books I published within a few years.

Publishing has always been somewhat opaque and often, as in 2009, disappointing in benefits and rewards. My personal feeling is that potential writers *write* and *do publish*, one way or another, doing so for the most part enjoyably. Of course, as André Gide says, "There is a lot of noise out there, and some of it is music."

To learn to read is life's beginning of a beautiful future with high degrees of enjoyment and happiness...with reading there are many doors open to a life unimaginably fulfilling!

A man who chooses not to read is just as ignorant as a man who cannot read.

> Mark Twain

John F. Kennedy read partly for information, partly for compassion, partly for insight, partly for the sheer joy of felicitous statement. He delighted particularly in quotations which distilled the essence of the argument.

DISPENSARY TO THE SOUL

> Inscription over the library at Trajan's Forum, Rome, Italy

You put enough individual enlightenment together and you get an enlightened society.

> Paul LeClerc, President, New York Public Library

The habit of reading is the only enjoyment in which there is no alloy; it lasts when all other pleasures fade.

> Anthony Trollope

What you read is more significant to your life than what you eat.

Peter Rabbit

When I was four years old, in 1926, my mother introduced me to the pleasure of her reading to me at our cottage in Babylon, Long Island. A favorite to hear was Beatrix Potter's illustrated The Tale of Peter Rabbit. *Mother seemed to enjoy these occasions as much as I did.*

After breakfast was the magical time for Peter Rabbit and his adventures along with Flopsy, Mopsy, and Cotton-Tail. I recall the repeated warnings of Mrs. Rabbit that her four young rabbits were not allowed to go into Mr. McGregor's garden! She cautioned: "Your father Rabbit had an accident there: he was put in a pie by Mrs. McGregor . . ." I remember that Peter Rabbit was very naughty, ran right away to Mr McGregor's garden, and squeezed under the gate!

My mother would raise her finger and say, raising her voice as well with a trembling question directed at me, "Whom should you, Peter Rabbit, *meet but Mr. McGregor!" . . . and so forth until the delightful tale was finished. I will never forget. Even to this day my grandchildren call me "Peter Rabbit" and beg me to read them the memorable* Tale of Peter Rabbit . . .

Your reading power at age eighty will tower over your reading power at age thirty.

Steve Leveen

Read in order to live.
> Gustave Flaubert

Truth is never out of print.

If you can read, you can cook.
> Alexandra Stoddard

Those who can read see twice as well.
> Menander

Isaac Watts concluded that reading is the most important method of self-improvement. Observation limits our learning to our immediate surroundings…reading alone allows us to reach out beyond the restrictions of time and space, to take part in the great conversation of ideas…no matter when or where we pursue it.
> Contributed by Susan Wise Bauer

The great interest in publishing is to take on an author at the start, or reasonably near it, and then to publish not this book or that, but the whole author.
> Maxwell Perkins (1930 letter)

Read Galsworthy's short story of young love, "The Apple-tree, the singing, and the gold." *See reference, Murray's Hippolytus of Euripides.*

All of us tend to become what we read and what we think. So be careful about our choices in what we do in both endeavors.

He smiled when he said to me, "Life is the thing, but I prefer reading."
> Logan Pearsall Smith

A room without books is like a body without a soul.
> Cicero

Only two classes of books are of universal appeal: the very best and the very worst.
> Ford Madox Ford

Take out of the library and read Omar Khayyam's Rubaiyat, *a Persian poem that warns of the dangers of greatness and the instability of fortune.*

Live always in the best company when you read.
> Sidney Smith

Reading is to the mind what exercise is to the body.
> Joseph Addison, *Tatler*, 1709-1711

A swami carried with him two books—the Bhagavad Gita *and the devotional classic,* The Imitation of Christ.

Lasting Gift by an Individual: Libraries

Steelman Andrew Carnegie persevered between 1902 and 1909 in creating 67 libraries in New York City—a total of 1600 libraries across the country. The result for America has been now recognized as astounding. Especially when we consider how the gift and values of one person can a century later shine in deeply rich ways for scores of years. My family visited the Carnegie library since the 1930s on Carnegie Hill at 96th Street between Park and Lexington.

Voltaire's whole program was a certain liberation of people through the critical process, the sifting of evidence, and that's what the library is all about.

WRITING

Writing can be an adventure, Winston Churchill conceded. Not always so: sent away from home in England at a young age, he actually struggled long with poor grades and compositions of his written work that drew extreme criticism from his unimpressed tutors. That is, until the exciting day he fell in love with words. He overcame an annoying lisp by meticulously reciting out loud to himself words and phrases that encouraged him in discovered self-importance and personal confidence.

He began to read a variety of books, especially histories of successful wartime battles of his ancestor (Marlborough) that deeply inflamed his imagination and, frustrated, led him to enter the British armed services in India and Africa and beyond. Instead of over-playing polo with fellow soldiers and imbibing gin and tonics in the barracks, he found for himself, quite suddenly, the growing pleasure of reading and writing. The key to this new adventure occurred while languishing in the army. He stumbled one afternoon on *Bartlett's Quotations*—this reference quote book became a heady fascination for him. He literally memorized

the book, reading page by page aloud to himself, while pretend-
ing to participate in historic battles and daring escapades with the
enemies abroad in exotic lands.

Soon Churchill was writing down episodes of his heavily fu-
eled imagination—making good use of *Bartlett's Quotations* and
his ancestor Marlborough who had distinguished himself in de-
feating Napoleon, who had seriously threatened the survival of
the British Empire. Writing became his major interest after reading. He took up professional journalism with both success and
bravado, while once combining all his talents in the Boer War and
fierce skirmishes in India and Africa. The journalist evolved into a
British war hero. He learned that his esoteric imagination could be
a wonderful source of fame and income. He wrote articles, essays and paid lectures, turned more lucratively to writing books;
then traveling widely and happily around the world—exponen-
tially increasing his heroic fame and his fortune. Churchill's smart
writing led to politics in Britain. He won a seat in Parliament, bring-
ing along every one of his talents, skills, vocabulary, and quirky
knowledge of the universe. In short time, Churchill became the
most famous person here and abroad. As they say, "the rest is
history"—World War I and II. Prime Minister of England . . . His
reading and writings provided the background for his extraordinary career in speaking in Parliament and publishing his writings
around the world, that had spearheaded his rise to immortality.

Edward Gibbon,
The Decline and Fall of the Roman Empire

Of the younger Gordian who ruled Rome more than a month in A.D. 238, Gibbon wrote, "Twenty-two acknowledged concubines and a library of sixty-two thousand volumes attested the variety of his inclinations, and from the productions which he left behind him, it appears that the former as well as the latter were designed for use rather than ostentation."

Beautiful, young Emily Webb in Thornton Wilder's high school play *Our Town* determines to go back to her grave to relive one day of her life in her folksy hometown, Grover's Corner. She exclaims, "Oh, earth, you're too wonderful for anyone to realize you!"
Simplicity is often sublime.

Big ideas are so hard to recognize, so fragile, so easy to kill. Don't forget that, all of you who don't have them.
John (Jock) Elliott, Jr.
Jock Elliott, Jr. was a master of words, phrases, ideas, and a fine and able human being and scholar: Santa Claus and slogans.

Ideas are to literature what light is to painting.
Paul Bourget

Henry David Thoreau never faltered. He was a born Protestant.
He declined to give up his large ambition of knowledge and action
for any narrow craft or profession, aiming at a much more comprehensive calling, *"the art of living well."*

Ralph Waldo Emerson

The world contrives to offer glittering prizes to those who have
stout hearts and sharp words.

F. E. Smith, the Earl of Birkenhead

To understand is to forgive.

Run your pen through every other word you have written; you
have no idea what vigor it will give your style.

Sidney Smith

Fifty years ago a young writer published his first novel.
Reviewers called it "disappointing" (The New Republic),
"phony" (Catholic World), "predictable" (The Nation). *The*
book: The Catcher in the Rye, *by J. D. Salinger!*

Poetry begins in emotion recollected in tranquility.

William Wordsworth

The childhood shows the man, as morning shows the day.

John Milton

The difference between the almost right word and the right word is really a large matter—it's the difference between the lightning bug and the lightning.

> Mark Twain

Just get it down on paper, and then we'll see what to do with it.

> Maxwell Perkins, legendary literary agent

Every artist writes his own autobiography.

> Havelock Ellis

Poetry occurs when the utmost reality and the utmost strangeness coincide.

> James Dickey

Bill paying and correspondence need constant attention; they stubbornly refuse to go away.

William F. Buckley, Jr. has some valuable advice for the new generation: how you say something is at least as important as what you say.

Midway in our life's journey, I went astray from the straight road and woke to find myself alone in a dark wood.

> Dante, 1300 A.D., first lines of the *Inferno*. Dante had a mid-life confusion. See his classic, *The Inferno* (*1300 A.D.*)

There is no there there.
> Gertrude Stein

All writers are a little crazy, but if they are any good they have a
kind of "terrible honesty."
> Raymond Chandler

A letter lights up the whole room. The epistolary art can still be
one of life's supreme joys.
> James Lord

A hand-written letter is a gift of kindness.

My schedule is flexible, but I am particular about my instruments:
lined index cards, well-sharpened, not too hard, No. 2 pencils
capped with erasers.
> Vladimir Nabokov

*He wrote entire books in pencil on index cards. Advice from
an accomplished writer. This book,* Figure It Out, *has been
initially composed by the author on index cards, totally
Nabokov's idea.*

*Surprisingly, your own vocabulary can be the measure of your
success in your life, career, happiness and desired love. Learn
early the music of words and phrases.* **This is the secret.**

Editing, as opposed to reading or writing: when done well, it's
invisible.
> Charles McGrath

Marcel Proust's ingenious writing was the constant attempt to "charge an entire lifetime with the utmost mental awareness."

Walter Benjamin

The next thing most like living one's life over again seems to be a recollection of that life, and to make that recollection as durable as possible by putting it down in writing.

Benjamin Franklin

I figured that the only thing that requires no education and no skills is writing.

Jessica Mitford

A cynic at work, who at thirty-eight decided to become a writer. Her book The American Way of Death (*1963*), *a scathing indictment of the American funeral industry, was immensely popular and brought her fame.*

Over 2400 years ago Plato wrote in the *Republic*, that if anyone at all is to have the privilege of lying, it should be the leaders of government.

Contributed by David Brinkley

Adam
Had 'em.

Strickland Gillilan

Said to be the shortest poem.

The memoir is the delight of two people—the author and his mother.

An old story, but the glory is forever.

> Virgil

Village

When Village: Where to Live and How to Live w*as published I was interested in any reader reaction, no matter how slight. One lady stopped me on the street to say how wonderful she thought it was. Very much pleased, I asked her why. "Oh," she said, "I'm nursing a baby, and your forty essays are each just short enough to complete by the time I'm finished."*

Speaking

If I am to speak for ten minutes, I need a week for preparation; if fifteen minutes, three days; if half an hour, two days; if an hour, I am ready now.

> Woodrow Wilson, former president

Preparation and timing of a speech are paramount for any success. President Wilson's advice is worthy. He deliberately talked his way into power.

I write only from my own experience. I write in blood, and the best truth is a bloody truth.

> Nietzsche

Suddenly one's thought or word disappears...The idea may come back or fade away or may be gone for all time. The best resolution is to grab the muse and write it down. Don't wait!

A grain of wit is more penetrating than the lightning of the nightstorm, which no curtains or shutters will keep out.

Ralph Waldo Emerson

Hollywood Dialogue

"Mr. Goldwyn, sir, I think this proposed movie script is too caustic!" "Well," Goldwyn replied [pause], "I don't care how much it costs..."

Public Speaking: Five Maxims

Public speakers should 1) study simplicity rather than grandiloquence, 2) indulge sparingly in purple patches, 3) avoid letting thoughts meander in unrelated, ill-ordered paths, 4) speak with considered emphasis on what is appropriate to the occasion, 5) and above all, sit down on expiration of allotted time.

Henry W. Taft, *Kindred Arts*,
(Macmillan Publishing Co.)

The job of the journalist is not to bring reality into line with appearances but to bring appearances into line with reality.

Michael Kinsley

The Elements of Style

Omit needless words. Vigorous writing is concise. A sentence should contain no unnecessary words, a paragraph; no unnecessary sentences, for the same reason that a drawing should have no unnecessary lines and a machine no unnecessary parts. This requires not that the writer make all his sentences short, or that he avoid all detail and treat his subjects only in outline, but that every word tell.

William Strunk, Jr.

Did you ever think of the rhythmical power of prose, how every writer when they get warm falls into a certain swing and rhythm peculiar to themselves, the words all having their place and sentences their cadences.

Harriet Beecher Stowe, letter to George Eliot

This word "now" is like a bomb thrown through the window, and it ticks.

Arthur Miller

Arthur Miller, of Death of a Salesman fame, onetime husband of Marilyn Monroe, hit the nail on the head with his choice quote on the dynamic word "now."

You write to me that it is impossible; the word is not French.

Napoleon, in a letter to General Lemarois, July 9, 1813

We have never had a formal rejection slip or letter to send out week after week to the many contributors who kindly send in notes or articles for consideration, and for whose work we sadly cannot or gladly do not want to find space, but we are encouraged to draft one, inspired by that used by the editors of a Chinese economics journal, and referred to in the *Times Diary*, 9 July 1982:

> We have read your manuscript with boundless delight. If we were to publish your paper it would be impossible for us to publish any work of a lower standard. As it is unthinkable that, in the next thousand years, we shall see its equal, we are, to our regret, compelled to return your divine composition, and to beg you a thousand times to overlook our short sight and timidity.
>
> Writing for Antiquity: An Anthology of Editorials from Antiquity

I beseech you in the bowels of Christ, think it possible you may be mistaken.

> Oliver Cromwell, from a saying that Judge Learned Hand would like to have written over the portals of every church, every school, every courthouse, and . . . of every legislative body in the United States

Summer afternoon—summer afternoon; to me those have always been the most beautiful words in the English language.

> Henry James

Wise leaders don't think abstractly. They use powers of close observation to integrate the vast shifting amalgam of data that constitute their own particular situation—their own and no other.

David Brooks

It takes a great deal of honesty to produce a little literature.

Henry James

Poetry enlivens our sense of beauty, sharpens our wits and stimulates our love of life and others.

The language of truth is always simple.

Seneca

A great flame follows a little spark.

Dante Alighieri, (1310-1321)
The Divine Comedy

"Did you see an old woman going down the path?" asks Bridget. "No, I did not," replies Patrick, who had just arrived after the old woman left, "But I saw a young girl," he said, "and she had the walk of a queen."

William Butler Yeats

The optimist as a poet.

All the good that gets done in this world is done by words.

Samuel Johnson

A word about Yeats: being Irish, he had an abiding sense of tragedy which sustained him through temporary periods of joy.

Literature is news that stays news.

Ezra Pound

Drama demands resolution in real life as well as fiction. Since the Greeks, dramatists have known that a good ending is one that acknowledges the longing of the audience for justice and the sense that order has been restored.

Lawrence Wright

Intellectuals live in their heads the way poets and serial killers do.

Peggy Noonan

Fiction lags after truth.

Edmund Burke, speech on conciliation
with America, 1775

A memoirist beneath whose pen truth became malleable as clay.

Letters are the great fixative of experience. Time erodes feeling. Time creates indifference. Letters prove to us that we once cared. They are the fossils of feeling. This is why biographers prize them so: they are biography's only conduit to unmediated experience. Everything else the biographer touches is stale, hashed over, told and retold, dubious, unauthentic…suspect.

Janet Malcolm

PHILOSOPHY

The philosophy which is so important in each of us is not a technical matter: it is our more or less dumb sense of what life honestly and deeply means. It is only partly got from books; it is our individual way of just seeing and feeling the total push and pressure of the cosmos.

William James

Often we come to a point in our lives when we dispense with the trivial and tire of ordinary superficialities. The idea literally intrudes on our meandering thinking to seriously focus on some study of philosophy that had, unfortunately, no part in much of our early education. Never too late?

By accepted definition, philosophy is the love of wisdom. What little I'd learned so far about this approach led me to believe that deeper knowledge of the meaning and purpose of life perhaps could bring about introspection and revelation for requisition through philosophy of a more perfect moral and rational existence *within ourselves.* This decision firmly made after completing Yale

89

Law School became a commitment that I've managed to keep up to the present day. The results to date are encouraging—I am reminded of Plato's remark to an old man who told him he was "attending classes on virtue." Plato looked him in the face and asked him sharply: "When will you finally begin to *live* virtuously?"

Plato and Aristotle were honest and philosophical teachers. They also enjoyed life, its ironies and amusements. But as Pascal, an ingenious philosopher himself, observed, both Plato and Aristotle philosophically lived simply, quietly, contemplatively. Thoreau, adopting a more critical tone, once remarked in his famous book, *Walden*, that "nowadays there are philosophy professors, but no philosophers. . . ."

I've especially enjoyed reading the enlightening words of Montaigne, who one day was told by a colleague, "I did nothing today." Montaigne exclaimed: "What? Did you not live? That is not only the most fundamental but the most illustrious of your occupations!"

I've learned a few things about philosophy, not much , but I have appreciated the clarity and wise words of Pierre Hadot, whose enlightening 2002 book *What Is Ancient Philosophy?* (Harvard University Press) is one of the best for a good educational introduction. This book has guided me to live a better way of life. It is a spiritual exercise essential in my mind for the attainment of wisdom as well as a sense of proportion.

Quotation of the Day (New York Times)

You want to know my philosophy? One day a peacock, the next day a feather duster.

> Pat Quinn, governor of Illinois, on his turn
> in the spotlight

To prize tranquility, to subdue pride…and not to dread an end that we share with everything in nature.

> Montaigne

The choice of a certain way of life…demands from the individual a total change of lifestyle, a conversion of one's entire being, and ultimately a certain desire to be and live in a certain way.

> Pierre Hadot

The philosopher's task is to create values.

> Friedrich Nietzsche

Nothing can bring you peace but yourself.

> Ralph Waldo Emerson

To be a philosopher is not merely to have subtle thoughts, nor even to found a school, but so to love wisdom as to live according to its dictates, a life of simplicity, independence, magnanimity, and trust.

> Henry David Thoreau

The proper study of mankind is man.

Alexander Pope

We think in generalities, but we live in detail.

Alfred North Whitehead

Better to live in generalities and think in detail.

Ancient Philosophy Summary
by Pierre Hadot

From the time of Socrates and Plato until the dawn of Christianity, philosophy always arose from an initial choice of a mode of life, from a panoramic vision of the universe, from a voluntary decision to experience the world along with other people, in a community or school.

Out of this conversion on the part of the individual emerged the philosophical discourse that would predicate representation of the world on the choice of a way of life. Ancient philosophy is thus not a system. It's a spiritual exercise that is essential for the attainment of wisdom.

No man is free who is not the master of himself.

Epictetus

The purpose of life seems to be to acquaint a man with himself.

Johann Wolfgang von Goethe

Thomas Jefferson's idea of an American aristocracy: Virtue and talents.

Michael Beschloss

The dignity of human life comes not from mere existence, but from that ability which separates us from the beasts, the ability to choose, freedom of will.

Immanuel Kant

A person cannot have complete understanding of the meaning of life. A person can only know its direction.

Leo Tolstoy

Enough of the Pluribus, for the moment; a little more of the Unum!

Lance Morrow

Enough about the many and more about the one.

The purpose of all civilization is to convert man, a beast of prey, into a tame and civilized animal, a domestic animal.

Nietzsche, The Genealogy of Morals (1887)

Our prejudices are too often a substitute for thinking.

The starry firmament above and the moral law within give me constant cause for wonder.

Immanuel Kant

To pay attention to this and ignore that—is to the inner life what choice of action is to the outer. In both cases, a man is responsible for his choice and must accept the consequences.

W. H. Auden

To thrive, intelligence must retain a relentless capacity for wonder. Napoleon's downfall began, as the poet Paul Valéry observed, when he was no longer astonished.

Edward Tenner

A man is not idle because he is absorbed in thought. There is a visible labor and there is an invisible labor.

Victor Hugo

Do not dismiss out of hand the opinion of your enemies. Your nemesis probably knows more about your faults than you do.

"What is truth?" said jesting Pilate, and would not stay for an answer.

Francis Bacon

A moment's insight can be equal to a lifetime of experience.

I never learn anything talking. I only learn things when I ask questions.

Lou Holtz

Vision is the art of seeing things invisible.
>
> Jonathan Swift

Excess is our ultimate enemy.

We can learn even from our enemies.
>
> Ovid

Each choice affects the universe.
>
> Kathy Steer Moor

How much easier it is to be critical than to be correct.
>
> Benjamin Disraeli

Revenge is the poor delight of little minds.
>
> Juvenal

Few people have the patience to stand by to hear the truth.

Life can only be understood backwards, but it must be lived forward.
>
> Soren Kierkegaard

Some of us spend endless time analyzing forward and living backward.

The strongest principle of growth lies in human choice.

T. S. Eliot when out of "The Wasteland" turned his poetry to the romance of Happiness for Two.

Untouched in the 1930s, a Colonial village filled with distinctive early Connecticut Valley houses shaded by huge elms and surrounded by field and woods...Two centuries of prosperity had given way to decline and depression which, in turn, had removed the financial ability of Deerfield's citizens to modernize their homes and surroundings. As a result, a corner of early New England was preserved pristine.

> Historic Deerfield
> Colonial village, the location of Deerfield
> Academy

All will be well, and all shall be well, and all manner of things shall be well.

> Julian of Norwich, 14th century mystic, and
> the first woman to be published in English

We have a world outside, a universe within.

> Jane Heap

Many a true word has been spoken in jest.

> Roxburghe Ballads (c. 1665)

Leisure with dignity.

> Cicero

No man's knowledge can go beyond his experience.

John Locke

And no man's experience can go beyond his knowledge.

Your choice determines your well-being, if not your success.

Once a word has been allowed to escape, it cannot be recalled.

Horace

The one thing the devil cannot bear is laughter.

HEROES

A miracle, a crash, and a new hero in our world

On Thursday, January 15th, 2009, a new hero suddenly appeared to capture the attention and imagination of the world. This hero was a handsome, well-trained U. S. Airways pilot, Chesley B. Sullenberger, III, captain of the plane, and a former Air Force Academy cadet.

Now fifty-seven, he took off from La Guardia Airport that afternoon for a short flight to Charlotte, North Carolina. Evidently, out of the blue-gray sky, flocks of birds extinguished both engines of the fifty-ton jet liner. This able pilot, his crew, and 155 passengers faced a total disaster. The only choice of action available in these dire circumstances, Sullenberger, in the blink of an eye, reasoned, was to descend over the Hudson River, gliding down to an emergency landing in the ice-cold water. Flight 1549 ditched into the river three and a half minutes after the engines lost power. The process of rescue of all passengers from their near-death experience was both traumatic and dramatic. On the surface of the Hudson, horrified passengers were scrambling out on the plane's wings, being picked up by an amazing flotilla of harbor vessels and small boats.

In these dreadful harrowing moments, an incredible miracle took place: Improbably, every single person survived—Captain Sullenberger retained his self-control throughout the turmoil of rescue. And afterwards he avoided the limelight and praise showered on him for his extraordinary feat. Most compelling to me was Captain Sullenberger's instant personal responsibility to save every passenger and crewmember, as when he twice checked the water-soaked cabin for stragglers before evacuating the sinking airplane himself. Once free to leave his plane, all aboard now rescued and safe, he fielded congratulatory phone calls from President Bush and President-elect Barack Obama on Friday, but mostly he stayed secluded somewhere in the city . . . He did not attend a ceremony at City Hall where Mayor Michael R. Bloomberg said his actions "inspired people all around the city, and millions more around the world."

Dr. Bruce Greyson, a professor of psychiatry, understood from empirical evidence that more positive near-death experiences tend to leave people with a sense of meaning and purpose in such a traumatic ordeal that, in general, can buffer long-term emotional distress, leaving them with a feeling of enhanced self-worth and a sense that they are not alone in dealing with life's traumas.

One day a little girl asked John F. Kennedy, "How did you become a war hero?" He replied, "Simple, young lady—they sank my boat."

Creed of a Hero

Think positively and masterfully with confidence and faith, and
life becomes more secure, more fraught with action, richer in
achievement and experience.

> Eddie Rickenbacker, World War I fighter
> pilot, hero unsurpassed

Each of us has some capacity for heroism.

> Charles Wells

*Often I think of other kinds of hero. That, it seems, should
not diminish the valiant airplane pilot or young soldiers in
Iraq. It can be—yes, even should be, at times—the courage,
vigor, and imagination of a five-year-old named Charlotte.
Picture the scene at a school play:*
Five-year-old Charlotte was the only grandchild not on stage.
When I asked what part she would play, I was told, "Oh, she's
the producer."

> Dee Hardie, from Thornhill Farm

A hero is no braver than an ordinary man, but he is brave five
minutes longer.

> Ralph Waldo Emerson

A hero does not die.

> Victoria Brynner

It is said that no man is a hero to his valet. That is because a hero can be recognized only by a hero.

Johann Wolfgang von Goethe

In the spring of 1927 Charles Lindbergh completed his solo flight to Paris (May 21, 1927). He said on arrival, "Well, here we are!" At the same time, I arrived at the top of Carnegie Hill, New York City, 1172 Park Avenue, at age five, escorted by my family. We all were awed by his daring and achievement, and still are.

A companion once said of the legendary Greek epic poet Homer:
"Seven cities claim great Homer dead/
Through which the ancient Homer begged his bread."
Homer is reported to have once mused, "To be a speaker of words and a doer of deeds, this is the quintessential victory of life."

LIFE

Man's real life is happy, chiefly, because he is ever expecting that it soon will be so.

Edgar Allen Poe, 1844-49

What is life but the short interval between birth and death? Contemplation of this quick period can produce many searching thoughts that can tantalize us, annoy us, cause us pain and suffering, and on some of those sublime occasions we know moments of happiness and joy . . . Seneca once said, "Life, if well used, is long enough!" "To contemplate human life," Marcus Aurelius mused, "for forty years is the same as contemplating it for ten thousand years. What more," he said, "will you see?"

Old sages, while engaged in deep contemplation, speculate that the utmost span of a man's life is a hundred years; they thought that half of it is spent at night, and of the rest, half is lost in childhood and old age; work, grief, longing and illness make up what may remain. Many philosophers like to show their gravitas by announcing to friend and foe that we are always *beginning to live*, but are never *living...*

I might conclude by saying that life is long to the miserable, but short to those who are happy. Now that I find myself approaching that remarkable age of nearing one hundred, I do confess to wishing an extension somehow, more time to be blessed with those golden hours with Alexandra where we live and love in those precious times together, sharing our deep affection for each other and our family, including its newest member, Cooper Lily Mott, three months old at this writing (February 2009).

Certainly, one thing is definite: our presence here on earth is finite. Now I understand the most important question affecting me is: how do I intelligently use, enjoy and savor with Alexandra the time we have left? I recall a certain walled garden in Beijing, China, near the Forbidden City, that had a writing on the wall. While visiting there one warm summer afternoon, I was surprised to read in bold yet graceful script the following message, quite distilled in English: "It is later than you think."

There are, to the optimist and the plucky, always new phases of life to live, to enjoy oneself and with others, providing more capital for our memory bank. Always growing, stretching ourselves, never becoming surfeited, leading to paralysis of personality . . . and happiness. The virtuous man or woman, Aristotle reminded us, is an active person.

Harvard professor Erik H. Erikson, in the ninth decade of his life, with his own beloved wife, Joan, tells us that lots of old people do not get wise—"But," he said, "you don't get wise *unless* you age." In later years, he sees the development of human interdependence. "Life doesn't make any sense without interdependence." His wife added, "We need each other, and the sooner we learn that, the better for us all."

Professor Erikson speaks poignantly of the wane of one's physical and sensory abilities at the end of life's journey. In that final period, we consciously reflect back over the course of our lives, comparing our dreams and hopes with the realities of what did happen; we learn the wisdom of humility, a realistic appreciation of our competence as well as our limits.

The Eriksons believe that wisdom has little to do with formal education. What is real wisdom? Wisdom, they agreed, comes from life experiences well digested. It's not what comes from [only] reading great books. When it comes to understanding life, "Experiential learning is the only worthwhile kind, everything else is hearsay." What the Eriksons seem to be telling us is: Live your life actively and deeply, think on those things that are lovely, true, and of good report, store up your memories in the banks of your mind (where thieves cannot break through and steal) and play back your recollections, creating a sense of completeness, of personal wholeness, strong enough to sustain us, in affectionate regard . . . til the end.

Let me assert my firm belief that the only thing we have to fear is fear itself—nameless, unreasoning, unjustified terror, which paralyzes needed efforts to convert retreat into advance.

Franklin D. Roosevelt

Aesop's Fly, sitting on the axle of the chariot, has been much laughed at for exclaiming: "What a dust I do raise!"

Thomas Carlyle

We are all prompted by the same motives, all deceived by the same fallacies, all animated by hope, obstructed by danger, entangled by desire and seduced by pleasure.

Samuel Johnson

What is life but love, tears, and cheers? And often besieged by some person's negative opinion . . .

Bob Hope Speaks

Today, my heart beat 103,389 times,
My blood traveled 168,000,000 miles,
I breathed 23,040 times,
I inhaled 438 cubic feet of air,
I spoke 4800 words, moved
750 major muscles, and I
Exercised 7,000,000 brain cells...
I'm tired!

Bob Hope

Life is on the high wire. All the rest is waiting.

Karl Wallenda, high wire artist

The desire of life prolongs it.
> Lord Byron

Live up your life while you're up and able.

Life feels shorter the better it is.

The signal of being a bore is to tell everything.

Lively and filled with interesting ideas.
> Brooke Astor, remarkable lady of
> character, who endorsed Alexandra's book
> *Living a Beautiful Life*

Brooke Astor deserves praise for her life of service to others and her kindness and charity to the general public. At the same time, she remained humble and gracious to all those around her. Her character and wisdom remained outstanding until she died. We shall always remember her excellent performance, her generosity and spirit-energy to the very end.

If something cannot go on, it will stop.

Don't follow your mentors, follow your mentors' mentors.
> David Leach

David Leach, wordsmith, coined the word chaordic—for complex systems that blend order and chaos.

Clear Up As You Go

Clutter is passé. So is a mess around your house.

As soon as a person asks himself the question "How do I live my life in the best way?," then all other questions are answered.

Leo Tolstoy

There is no such thing as pure pleasure; some anxiety always goes with it.

Ovid

Our body is precious. It is our vehicle for awakening. Treat it with care.

Buddha

Life is neither suffering nor pleasure, but the business we have to do, and which we have to finish honestly, up to our life's end.

Alexis de Tocqueville

The good things of life are not to be had singly, but come to us with a mixture.

Charles Lamb

They come, I suppose, as in-laws and trailing uninvited guests.

Don't take my Zen away from me!

Brooke Stoddard

No life is more interesting than any other life; everybody's life takes place in the same twenty-four hours of consciousness and sleep; we are all locked into our own subjectivity, and who is to say that the thoughts of a person gazing into the vertiginous depths of a volcano in Sumatra are more objectively interesting than those of a person trying on a dress at Bloomingdale's?

      Janet Malcolm

The only thing that keeps a man going is energy. And what is energy but liking life?

      Louis Auchincloss

Life is painting a picture, not doing a sum.

      Justice Oliver Wendell Holmes, Jr.

Change and strife are the natural conditions of the universe. This is why we should embrace them both.

Reasoning, tested by doubt, is argumentation. In developing our argument we too often forget what argument is designed to do. Nietzsche taught us, "The most fundamental form of human stupidity is forgetting what we were trying to do or say in the first place."

Self-preservation is the most basic instinct of all sentient beings.

      Sherwin B. Nuland, M.D.

When you are hungry you are losing weight.

Discipline requires, every time, experiencing the hard and necessary before the soft and easy.

There is no new thing under the sun.
                    Ecclesiastes 1:9, c. 200 B.C.
Yet we go every day thinking there is.

The sure way to get a thing done is to do it now—yourself.

Intemperance is an intemperant disease, unfortunately rarely cured.

The more I study the world, the more I am convinced of the inability of brute force to create anything durable.
                    Napoleon Bonaparte
A most unexpected saying from the tyrant Napoleon.

My formula for living is quite simple. I get up in the morning, and I go to bed at night, between I occupy myself as best I can.
                    Cary Grant

In respect to foresight and firmness, the people are more prudent, more stable, and have better judgment than Princes.
                    Niccolò Machiavelli

Think probabilistically. While no one can predict the future, it is possible to assess the odds of various futures.

The moral for modern man is clear. He has a duty to nourish those qualities within himself that make him a free and morally responsible being. And he has an equally compelling duty to honor values beyond the self.

Judge Learned Hand

What has long been true but too often forgotten is that every person needs and appreciates encouragement, rather than criticism.

Be careful what you give up.

Eleanor McMillen Brown

There is no little enemy.

Benjamin Franklin

Human nature remains the same, but our options for good—and ill—increase.

Richard Brookhiser

You never know.

Bishop John Bowen Coburn

Intellectual play, like the play of childhood, is a serious business.
                    Kay Redfield Jamison

A sense of humor is a sense of proportion.

Coincidence proves nothing—but itself. You don't have to think any more about it.

My salad days; when I was green in judgment.
                    William Shakespeare

In human relations, silence and avoidance are tools of greatest cruelty—and insult.

A good neighbor increases happiness.

When you make a mistake, recognize that you've made a mistake, and try to turn heat into light.
                    Lawrence H. Summers

Live like the strings of a fine instrument—not too taut and not too loose.
                    Buddha

Every morning is not a new day, but a new life and a new chance.
                    David Lloyd George

Yes, one of the brightest gems in the New England weather is the dazzling uncertainty of it all.

        Mark Twain

Give the people what they want to see and they will come.

        Favorite aphorism of controversial Holly-
        wood movie mogul Harry Cohn—which
        became the constant explanation for his
        crowded funeral

Wolves and swans mate for life. Is there a lesson there?

Do not seek to have events happen as you want them to, but instead want them to happen as they do happen, and your life will go well.

        Epictetus

Dwell on this conception of Epictetus for your own harmony and peace of mind.

One should not always think so much about what one should do, but neither what one should be. Our works do not ennoble us; but we must ennoble our works.

        Meister Eckhart

To be told is not equal to the experience.

        Maxim conveyed by a Mystic, Connecticut
        Yellow Cab driver

You can run, but you can't hide.

> Brooke Stoddard

When you come back to a project after a time lapse you find the situation opaque, as though you were looking through a shadow. Good reason to go the extra mile while you're on the way.

It is a very noble hypocrisy not to talk of one's self.

> Friedrich Nietzsche

Every task worth doing deserves your care.

I think that, as life is action and passion, it is required of a man that he should share the passion and action of his time at peril of being judged not to have lived.

> Justice Oliver Wendell Holmes, Jr.

This is the one true joy in life: the being used for a purpose recognized by yourself as a mighty one.

> George Bernard Shaw

We're all on a journey but many of us on different paths— some toward truth, love, and beauty, others toward misery, hatred, and oblivion. Choice becomes pivotal on our way to happiness.

Life wastes itself while we are preparing to live.
Ralph Waldo Emerson

In our daily lives and human conflicts we should strive to learn early on the supreme defensive measure of "playing dumb," also described as being "cunningly naïve." Try out this disarming technique without embarrassment or regret.

Our judgments about things vary according to the time left us to live.
André Gide

"Almost everything in life happens by chance," novelist William Trevor observed. "[People] miss a train and a person's life changes."

This is the best day the world has ever seen. Tomorrow will be better.
R. A. Campbell

Give us grace and strength to forebear and to preserve… Give us courage and gaiety and the quiet mind.
Robert Louis Stevenson

Neurosis is just a high-class word for whining.
Albert Ellis
Whining is not winning.

A friend said one night while we were talking calmly about what's going on in the world: The first half of life I was encouraged to speak up for common sense. Now, the second half, I'm told, "Don't you dare!"

We make a living by what we get, we make a life by what we give.

Winston Churchill

Whether we're aware or not, all creatures are connected. We are inseparably bonded together, a realization that grows stonger each day.

Man is the only animal that blushes, or needs to.

Mark Twain

Once on the Central Park merry-go-round you and your child have only one chance to catch the golden ring. This is true of life itself. So teach the child to be alert and not let the golden ring go by, forever lost…go for it!

Each life converges to some center.

Emily Dickinson

The Aim, reached or not, makes great the life.

Robert Browning

I like the dreams for the future better than the history of the past.
Thomas Jefferson

Little things affect little minds.
Benjamin Disraeli

No man ever becomes great by imitation.
Samuel Johnson

The longer I live, the more things I must complete.
William Ellery Channing

Hard work never killed anybody, but why take a chance?
Charlie McCarthy (Edgar Bergen)

Chinese Village Song by Theresa Teng

The Story of a Little Village
Many are the stories of a small village
Full of joy and happiness.
If you came to this little village,
How much you would reap;
It looks like a painting,
It sounds like a song.

Life is a struggle.
Euripides

A little integrity is better than a career.

> Ralph Waldo Emerson

Any integrity is better than anything else.

What we least expected generally happens.

> Benjamin Disraeli

The real difference between genius and stupidity is that genius has its limits.

No good deed goes unpunished.

> Old adage (contributed by Mayor John
> V. Lindsay)

Life has had more than three billion years to evolve on earth, complex life a billion years, a million years that it took mankind to reach its present stage of evolution.

> Steven Pinker

It is best to win without fighting.

> Sun-Tzu

This brilliant strategy—to succeed—takes more skill, experience, and diplomacy than fighting outright. Sun-Tzu had this rare Chinese general's genius.

The total bother of one buzzing fly.

Most people have an insatiable desire to be right.

Carl Jung as psychiatrist speaks of the curve of a lifetime being divided in half: the first half is the time of relation-ships, the second half is finding the sense of one's life within, *following the footsteps of the human experience one has had with one's inward life. And finally total disengagement, go-ing through the last passage without anxiety and without fear. The better your imagination, the better your mind can take you on magical travels and wonderful experiences.*

Aversion is the flip side of desire.

First the famine, then the feast.
> Bishop Fulton Sheen, *opening words,*
> *St. Bartholomew's Church sermon*

It isn't the size of the dog in the fight that counts, it's the size of the fight in the dog.

Wouldn't the social fabric come undone if we were wholly frank to everyone?
> Ingmar Bergman, *The Misanthrope*

We go back and back, forever; we go back all of us to the very beginning…We cannot understand all of the traits we have inher-ited. Sometimes we can be strangers to ourselves.
> V. S. Naipaul

TRAVEL

Travel is the front door of freedom. Most of us nowadays would run out of conversation should we stop traveling anywhere. From September of 1929 to January of 1943, presumably because of the Great Depression, my whole family ceased traveling outside the United States until we all took a month's holiday in Bermuda in 1937, just made possible by a small inheritance from my grandfather's death. We loved every minute.

World War II shook up travelicity in spades. Seemingly everyone was traveling . . . Soon, as a practicing lawyer and former prosecutor in New York City I learned that judges took their holidays regularly in August. This revelation led to my inviting Alexandra and our children to take our travel holiday in August as well—and somewhat inspired, we all traveled that month to France, Bermuda, Italy, what was then the Soviet Union, China, Hawaii, Belgium, and many other countries in the following years.

Face it: travel has been healthy, happy, and lots of fun (arguably less so today . . .). We still equate travel with fun and continue the endless conversation with such discussion weekly as "Where are we going to travel this year?" Travel remains intriguing—you never know what will happen.

For my part, I travel not to go anywhere, but to go. I travel for travel's sake. The great affair is to move.

Robert Louis Stevenson

Despite our natural ebullience there are limitations we must reluctantly recognize: We have just so much time, so many resources, so much stamina and endurance. Within these limits, we bravely carve out our destiny . . . and our precious travel time.

Experiencing rain in Paris is a delight; seldom elsewhere.

On being urged to see pyramids in the Egyptian desert: Worth seeing? Yes, but not worth *going* to see.

Samuel Johnson

If you love Paris, go.

Brooke Stoddard

PRIVACY

Aside from the recent study and interpretation of constitutional law regarding the blossoming interest in privacy, there is, or should be, a general and personal consideration of this sensitive, necessary issue—our own privacy needs and obligations toward others. First, most of our friends, family, associates, and companions seem to have developed, on their own initiative, a strong feeling of personal desire to achieve an outright need for their own privacy, whether at home, on vacation, while traveling, retail shopping, going to the theater, dealing with employees or any other persons who may seek personal matters that may affect us or impact us in any way.

This new level of privacy is growing in the new world of mass consciousness of the sacred nature of our own identity. In other words, can we, if we wish, be *personally* private with commensurate benefits and protection? I do think the time has come to give people personal rights to privacy—the right to live privately, as they wish, at all times, day and night, wherever they choose to be. Personal privacy may be considered a more comprehensive right of privacy—and the right most valued by civilized men and women in future days ahead. *Privacy*—just the sound of the word gives us an exhilarating feeling of confidence, hope, and high spirits about the right to be left alone, without unwarranted intrusion by government, media, or other institutions or pesky individuals.

We can recall that it was not until the U.S. Supreme Court decision in *Griswold* v. *Connecticut* (1965) which voided a state statute preventing the use of contraception, that the modern doctrine of privacy emerged. In his opinion, Justice William O. Douglas argued that a protection from intrusion into marital privacy was a constitutional right, a *penumbra* (partial shadow) emanating from the specific guarantees of the Constitution. The right to sexual privacy as set forth in *Griswold* v. *Connecticut* was one of the main foundations of the court's decision in *Roe* v. *Wade* (1973) to overturn state abortion statutes. All recently confirmed justices to the Supreme Court have affirmed their belief in the right to privacy.

More than 100 years ago the Supreme Court Justice-to-be Louis Brandeis and his former law professor, Samuel Warren, published an original perspective article for the Harvard Law Review. *They argued that the common law secures to each individual the right of determining ordinarily to what extent his thoughts, sentiments, and emotions shall be communicated to others. During the past century, and especially today, this perceived right of privacy has faded away in the frenzy of the information age.*

To me, privacy is the most valuable asset that money can buy.
Paul Mellon

"Love, like happiness, evokes an abundance of ecstasy," Paul
Mellon said, "intensely satisfying and joyful." Among the things he
adored, he listed the sound of birds, the smell of flowers, the taste
of "the evening's first cold and dry martini," and "perhaps the
most important, the thrill and mystery of touching, of love between a man and a woman." Paul Mellon required excellence in
all things. He believed knowledge of the best, from his personal
experience, inspires people to seek the best in themselves. Here
is one key to happiness.
John Russell, quoting Paul Mellon's obituary
in the *New York Times*, February 3rd, 1999

*A note on privacy—keep your records, journals, and diaries
close at hand, and out of other hands...evade identity theft, a
wicked burgeoning bother.*

Civilization is the progress toward a society of privacy. The
savage's whole existence is public, ruled by the laws of his or her
tribe. Civilization is the process of setting man free.
Ayn Rand, *The Fountainhead*, 1943

Everyone, host and guest alike, welcomes privacy.
Billy Baldwin

Privacy is a badge of freedom.

SUCCESS

I was recently asked by an old friend at lunch if I had found my life—so far—to have been a "success." I tried to defend myself by saying I was asked a tough question that relied on a correct definition of "success," if there is one . . . That evening I began to dwell on his question. In today's world, is there a fair and reasonable answer? Would my response amount to biting into cotton candy—a bit sweet, yet of no consequence? I decided to attempt to figure it out in words as honest as possible. Here are the notes I sent on to my friend:

So-called success in life is apt to be an illusion for most of us. Personally, my success in life is my happiness with Alexandra during the past 35 years of marriage. We are living the good life, completely, first in New York City and now in Stonington Village, Connecticut, together with our children and grandchildren. We particularly enjoy walking about the village (no car), working on the renovation of our eighteenth-century cottage, taking short trips abroad together, visiting museums . . . Alexandra and I set up writing rooms in the cottage where we contrive to write books side by side. When available we enjoy abundant sunshine out-of-doors, with new lighting throughout the cottage. In the village, we daily visit great restaurants happily serving delicious fresh food, cooked by our chef friends. We're surrounded by our Roger Mühl painting collection throughout the cottage to inspire us and celebrate his memory. We value time reading great literature; we receive contentment, illumination, and peace of mind.

We treasure our privacy with no interruptions. In the evenings we like to sit by cozy fires listening to favorite music; sharing our ideas, hopes, and dreams about future days together; savoring a sip of New Zealand Marlborough wine; welcoming the visits of our newest granddaughter Cooper, who just arrived in the world, adding joy to our evolving family. We celebrate our friends from near and far. I particularly enjoy writing letters, communicating with these friends going back over half a century. Also working with New York City's police officers and firefighters and their families has enriched my life for over sixty years; I do wish to continue these endeavors as long as I live.

Alexandra and I plan as many days as possible of simplicity and quiet in order to do our work; we arrange to have spring flowers in our cottage to cheer us the year around with happiness and love; we surround ourselves with clean, fresh colors in our cottage and are grateful for our small flower garden in back of the cottage, overlooking Little Narragansett Bay and Stonington Village Harbor, where children regularly ply the waters in eager summer races—with flags flying! We take pleasure in the outdoor shower in the Zen garden overlooking our forest of Nikko Blue hydrangea.

There's never a day we don't appreciate the beauty of nature in this small fishing village we've chosen as our home. When our daughter Alexandra was at Connecticut College, in nearby New London, Connecticut, she sent us a short essay by Ralph Waldo Ralph Waldo Emerson that touched us with its exceptional sentiment and truth. Years later, Alexandra included Ralph Waldo Emerson's words on success in her book *Making Choices: The Joy of a Courageous Life*, and when her brother Powell died in Chicago during open-heart surgery, she recited this essay on success in her eulogy at her brother's memorial service. These eloquent words of Ralph Waldo Emerson about living a successful, happy life continue to ring true to me to this day.

To laugh often and much, to win the respect of intelligent people and the affection of children, to earn the appreciation of honest critics and endure the betrayal of false friends, to appreciate beauty, to find the best in others, to leave the world a bit better, whether

by a healthy child, a garden patch . . . to know even one life has breathed easier because you have lived. This is to have succeeded!
Ralph Waldo Emerson

Those who make no errors never make anything at all.

For a lively mind, work and creativity are continuous.

When you come back to a project after a time lapse you find the situation opaque, as though you were looking through a shadow. Good reason to go the extra mile while you're on the way.

What the mind cries out for is serious work that alone furnishes the risk, the reward, the new experience that a living spirit must have or perish.
Michael Drury

Concentration is everything. On the day I'm performing, I don't hear anything anyone says to me.
Luciano Pavarotti

Design the work
Then work your design.

Your backup plan can diminish disappointment.

The best executive is the one who has enough sense to pick good men to do what he wants done and self-restraint enough to keep from meddling with them while they do it.

> Theodore Roosevelt

Just keep to an even course.

> Molière, *Le Juste Milieu*

The Pedigree of Honey
Does not concern the Bee—
A Clover, any time,
Is Aristocracy.

> Emily Dickinson

Sticking to it is the genius.

> Thomas Edison

Work, work, work is the main thing.

> Abraham Lincoln, on becoming a lawyer, in a letter dated September 25th, 1860, to a young schoolteacher who inquired about how to learn the law

Victory at all costs, victory in spite of all terror. Victory however long and hard the road may be, for without victory there is no survival.

> Winston Churchill

The healthiest competition occurs when average people put in above-average effort.

General Colin Powell

General Colin Powell has shown brilliant effort in a lifetime of service. He deserves high respect and praise. During the huge regalia of the Barack Obama inaugural, January 20th, 2009, Colin Powell inspired thousands of people with his eloquence and common sense. At one time he was considered a top candidate for president.

If A is a success in life, then A equals X plus Y plus Z. X is work, Y is play, and Z is keeping your mouth shut.

Albert Einstein

To burn always with this hard gemlike flame, to maintain this ecstasy, is success in life.

Walter Pater

Success rarely brings total satisfaction.

Along with success comes a reputation for wisdom.

The sublime, introduced at the right moment, carries all before it with the rapidity of lightening and reveals at a glance the mighty power of genius.

Longinus

Do what you can, with what you've got, where you are!
>> Theodore Roosevelt

The leader of the free world, a valiant general and Supreme Commander of World War military and naval forces. His biography reviews with great style his outstanding career and personality.

No one can defeat us unless we first defeat ourselves.
>> Dwight D. Eisenhower

It is no use saying "We are doing our best." You have got to succeed in doing what is necessary.
>> Winston Churchill

I love fools' experiments, I am always making them.
>> Charles Darwin

There is no large and difficult task that can't be divided into little, easy tasks.
>> Buddhist saying

Do small things as if they were great...and great things as if they were small and easy.
>> Blaise Pascal

Noble people rejoice in the happiness and success of others.
>> A. B. Stoddard

The majority of people want to do something unusual and difficult in order to improve their lives, but they would do better to purify their wishes, and improve their inner selves.

Leo Tolstoy

Working on our inner selves is the primary road to enlightenment.

We are what we believe we are.

U.S. Supreme Court Justice Benjamin N. Cardozo

The moral flabbiness born of the exclusive worship of the bitch-goddess SUCCESS. That—with the squalid cash interpretation put on the word success—is our national disease.

William James, in a letter to H. G. Wells, September 11th, 1906

William James, with his inquiring mind, turned the world around with his writing on the new science of psychology.

Perseverance—a prime tool of success.

Alexandra Stoddard

There is no comparison between that which is lost by not succeeding and that which is lost by not trying.

Contributed by Natalie Sherman and inspired by Sir Francis Bacon

Those who know how to win are much more numerous than those who know how to make proper use of their victories.

Polybius (c. 200-118 B.C.)

To persist in or remain constant to a purpose, idea, or task in spite of obstacles. [Latin perseveres—very serious.]

Success is going from failure to failure without loss of enthusiasm.

Winston Churchill

Always do right. This will gratify some people, and astonish the rest.

Mark Twain

Greatness Defined

To endure is greater than to dare;
To tire out hostile fortune;
To be daunted by no difficulty;
To keep heart when all have lost it;
To go through intrigue spotless;
To forgo even ambition when the end is gained.
Who can say this is not greatness?

William Makepeace Thackeray,
Prime Minister of England, (1811-1863)

I owe all my success in life to having been always a quarter of an hour beforehand.

Lord Nelson

An expert is one who knows more and more about less and less.
> Nicholas Murray Butler

Butler was president of Columbia University, where he made this remark in a commencement address.

James Watson, co-discoverer of DNA, had his own Fourth Rule for How to Succeed in Science*: "Have fun and stay connected. Never do anything that bores you."*

There is no absolute formula for success.
> Jamel Oeser-Sweat, age 17, nationwide Westinghouse Science Talent Search Scholarship winner

If I have seen further it is because I have stood on the shoulders of giants.
> Isaac Newton

Success follows a focused career.

In most situations, when you change one thing, you have to rethink everything.
> Alexandra Stoddard, *who learned this wisdom from Eleanor McMillen Brown, her gracious mentor and friend*

Exuberance increases risk-taking, innovative thinking and the anticipation of success.
> Dr. Samuel Barondes

The Amazing Disappointments:
Lincoln's Failures

*When Abraham Lincoln was a young man he ran the legisla-
ture in Illinois and was badly swamped. He next entered business, failed, and spent 17 years of his life paying off the debts
of a worthless partner. He fell in love with a beautiful young
woman to whom he became engaged—then she died. Enter-
ing politics, he ran for Congress and was badly defeated. He
then tried to get an appointment to the United States Land
Office, but failed. He became a candidate for the United States
Senate and was badly defeated. In 1856 he became a candidate for the vice presidency and was again defeated. In 1858
he was defeated by Douglas. But in the face of all these de-
feats and failures, he eventually achieved the highest success
attainable in life, and undying fame to the end of time, and
the continuing admiration and respect of young and old.*

If one advances confidently in the direction of his dreams, and
endeavors to live the life which he has imagined, he will meet with
a success unexpected in common hours. If you have built castles
in the air, your work need not be lost; that is where they should
be! Now put the foundations under them.
                    Henry David Thoreau

Every calling is great when greatly pursued.
                    Oliver Wendell Holmes, Sr.

The key goals of success are to be able to plan ahead, to envision consequences and exercise the true gifts of your free will.

To succeed you must add water to your wine, until there is no more wine.

Jules Renard

Even with hard work and discipline, success for any of us can be both elusive and transitory, especially in bad times. How can we engage ourselves with the Greek principles comprising work, wisdom, passion and virtue they called eudaemonia—a happy balancing with service to others?

Work, wisdom, and passion, and the greatest of these is wisdom, because wisdom is the love of truth and truth is the prize.

HISTORY

Basically history is no more or less than a narrative of past events, perhaps a story of chronology, a branch of knowledge that records in various ways and sometimes benefits us by analysis of past activities. We like to think that history can repeat itself in endless cycles (how accurately I'm afraid we can't be sure . . .).

One example may suffice to illustrate why our belief about the quixotic nature of history can be considered somewhat wobbly. My father left a job in Cleveland, Ohio, as an assistant manager of the Aluminum Company of America. He came to realize that the position at that time (the late 1920s) was somewhat of a dead end for him. This outlook accounted for his decision to accept an offer from his friend and former roommate at Yale (class of 1914/15), Francis Thorne, to join his well-regarded brokerage firm in New York City. The timing seemed propitious, at least until September 1929, when the stock market suddenly crashed, continuing to plunge down for more than a decade—a distressing period soon labeled the Great Depression, relieved only in the months after by the pounding activities of the Second World War.

During this awful recession my father found there was no Wall Street business. He would come home early to find me also at home, having arrived from the Browning School earlier. This coincidence led my father to call me into the library of our apartment at 1172 Park Avenue, where he would direct me to sit down and listen to his recital of what catastrophe was going on "downtown on Wall Street." Day after day, I learned more about such arcane economics than I cared to know. Several years later, his repeated instruction took on a rhythm of truth, meaning, and purpose. This was not a pitty-pat "depression," he said, it was a "recession," causing deep pain and suffering to millions, growing worse every week, in every way, throughout the globe. There was no relief and no available support for the tragic hardships that descended upon virtually everyone. To understand what happened in those desperate years of the Great Depression is to simply observe what has occurred in the current years of 2007-2010. The similarities are striking.

The stress and strain of these events, in my opinion, caused my father's early death in 1946 at the young age of fifty-four. Until his untimely death he had long held the oldest track record for the half mile at Yale, unbroken to this day. The Great Depression had taken its toll, totally.

Evolution is a sequence of accidents. Its path is as unpredictable as the trajectory of a pinball. No wonder sophisticated intelligence has developed only once in two billion years.

David Papineau

From his bully pulpit, Teddy Roosevelt spoke out with keen directions to do not only our best but what Winston Churchill called our "necessary" duty.

We make war that we may live in peace.
>   Aristotle

France was long a despotism tempered by epigrams.
>   Thomas Carlyle

It is said an Eastern monarch once charged his wise men to invent him a sentence to be ever in view, and which should be true and appropriate in all times and situations. They presented him the words: "And this, too, shall pass away."
>   Abraham Lincoln

Reading David McCullough's book 1776 is a tonic: "The year 1776, celebrated as the birth year of the nation and for the signing of the Declaration of Independence, was, for those who carried the fight for independence forward, a year of all too few victories, of sustained suffering, disease, hunger, desertion, cowardice, disillusionment, defeat, terrible discouragement, and fear, as they would never forget, but also phenomenal courage and bedrock devotion to country, and that, too, they would never forget . . . the outcome seemed little short of a miracle."

When President Nixon ordered U.S. Attorney General Elliot
Richardson to fire Watergate Special Prosecutor Archibald Cox
during the Saturday Night Massacre, Richardson had refused
and resigned. In his office at the Justice Department,
Richardson picked up the phone and called Cox. Both
Richardson and Cox understood the ethics of ancient Greeks,
as well as being believers in the rule of law. At that point,
Richardson read to Cox from Homer:

> *Now, though numberless fates of death beset us*
> *Which no mortal can escape or avoid:*
> *Let us go forward together, and either*
> *We shall give honor to one another*
> *Or another to us.*

William Ellery Channing, 1780-1842, American Unitarian
minister and author, b. Newport, RI. At twenty-three ordained
minister of the Federal Street Congregational Church in Bos-
ton, where he served until his death. He was a leader among
those who were turning from Calvinism. Known as the
"apostle of Unitarianism," he led the formation of the Ameri-
can Unitarian Association. His plea was for humanitari-
anism and tolerance in religion rather than a new creed.
Not only a great preacher but a lucid writer, he influenced
many American authors including Ralph Waldo Emerson and
other Transcendentalists and Holmes and Bryant. He was
ahead of his time. (See The Philosophy of William Ellery
Channing *by R. L. Patterson, 1952, reprinted 1972.)*

Mahatma Gandhi, observing the world, made it clear: "There is more to life than increasing its speed." Gandhi, the great Indian prime minister, was a thoughtful, courageous philosopher of life. He was assassinated in 1948, in a surprise attack, for political reasons.

At the very end, the great philosopher and statesman Cicero was pursued by assassins. He felt weary of both flight and life itself. At the same time, according to Robert Wilkin, Cicero realized that a number of virtuous men had met a similar fate. One example was the trial and sentence to death of Socrates in Athens. He figured that these horrifics are "fate," and as such may even be considered for the best.

We know how to save the Union. In giving freedom to the slave, we assure freedoms to the free. Honorable alike in what we give and what we preserve, we shall nobly save, or meanly lose, the last best hope of Earth.

> Abraham Lincoln, address to Congress, December 1862

Any song, says Jelly Roll Morton, can be played as "blues" or "joys." Ferdinand Joseph La Menthe, known as "Jelly Roll Morton" (1885-1941): American musician and composer who recorded seminal jazz works during the 1920s and claimed to have invented jazz.

Charles Darwin, reports Adam Gopnik, was a craftsman of huge resource and a great deal of "quiet mischief." "Our descent [in evolution] is the origin of our evil passions!" Darwin said. ". . . The Devil under form of Baboon is our grandfather!"

Let us have faith that right makes might, and in that faith let us to the end dare to do our duty as we understand it.

Abraham Lincoln, address at Cooper Union,
New York City, February 27th, 1860

Alexandra and I attended an exact replay at the exact location at Cooper Union.

General Patton spoke with keen energy to the soldiers of the Normandy invasion army in World War II, a famous, now faded away, piece of history. "Courage and personal responsibility involves each one of us. Play one's part and contribute to the whole effort: don't ever let up. Don't ever think your job is unimportant. Every man has a job to do and he must do it. He is a vital link in a great chain. What would our country, our loved ones, our homes, even the world be like to ignore our duty? No, Americans don't think like that. Every man does his job. Every man serves the whole!"

The three essentials of Napoleon's style in the field, Charles de Gaulle said in The Edge of the Sword, *were "to grasp the situation, to adapt himself to it, and to exploit it to his own advantage."*

Yale Class of 1944:

Remarks of the Master of Ceremonies, Fifty-Fifth Class Reunion (1999)

Welcome to the fifty-fifth annual reunion dinner of the renowned class of 1944—a wartime class. We gathered—carefree and innocent—on the Old Campus in September 1940 just after the fall of France…We had little idea what struggles, losses, joys and friendships lay ahead. A year later, Pearl Harbor was our wakeup call. Classmates immediately started to volunteer for war service; many more followed. At the war's end thirty-six of our classmates did not survive to come home again.

This separation created an unconscious covenant among us, forging an unusual harmony of spirit and friendship continuing to this day. For this we think our class is envied—or ridiculed—by other Yale classes for our exceptionally high regard for ourselves, for record fundraising, high government service, achievements over the years in many fields.

Better than any other class? Classmate Knobby Walsh says "Yes." Our good friend Stu Little, more restrained, said, "It is an arguable point. . . ."

Now, here today, we are across from the Old Campus—125 of the surviving 1944 classmates—celebrating with spouses and family and friends a roller-coaster time in a tumultuous world, still full of surprises and wars, still replete with periods of joy and happiness.

Perseverance and spirit have done wonders in all ages.
George Washington

Franklin Delano Roosevelt, our four-term president, referred to as FDR, kept a sign over his White House desk during the Great Depression years. His visitors looked into these words:
LET UNCONQUERABLE GLADNESS DWELL
FDR conquered a severe personal handicap from polio and overcame with enormous faith and optimism. His spirit-energy of survival and public service is remembered as renowned and unique in the quality of his leadership.

Witness the scene of a lively symposium of illustrious souls gathered together one evening. The noise of conviviality and laughter rises . . . Suddenly Judge Learned Hand raises his hand, jumps up from his chair onto a table and shouts: "Shut up, Voltaire! I want to speak!"

In its 4.5 billion years of existence, Earth has withstood deep cold that nearly turned the entire planet into a ball of ice and blazing heat that opened the Arctic to alligators and other warm-weather creatures.
Front page, *International Herald Tribune,* December 1st, 1997

Experience is helpful, but it is judgment that matters.
General Colin Powell

Inferiors revolt in order that they may be equal, and equals that they may be superior. Such is the state of mind that creates revolutions. In revolutions the occasions may be trifling, but great interests are at stake.

Aristotle

Adlai Stevenson, defeated by Dwight Eisenhower for President, was asked by a woman how he felt giving his concession speech. He quickly replied: "I'm reminded of what Abraham Lincoln said after an unsuccessful election—that he felt like a little boy who had stubbed his toe in the dark. He said that he was 'too old to cry, but it hurt too much to laugh.'"

Calvin Coolidge, the taciturn 30th U.S. President in the lively 1920s, left for church one Sunday in his New England village. When he returned home, his wife asked him, "Calvin, how was the clergyman's sermon?" "Okay," he said. "What did he preach about?" "Sin," he replied. "What did he have to say about it?" she inquired. The president looked up from his paper. "He's agin it."

At six feet eight inches, economist laureate John Kenneth Galbraith always exhibited huge self-assurance. When he once complained to President Kennedy that he didn't see why the New York Times had to call him "arrogant," Kennedy replied, "I don't know why not, Ken. Everybody else does."

The American Indians had no laws, no punishments, and no government. They obeyed the moral understanding of good and evil that is part of every human nature.

Thomas Jefferson

I sought for the greatness and genius of America in her commodious harbors and ample rivers, and it was not there; in her fertile fields and boundless prairies, and it was not there; in her rich mines and her vast world commerce, and it was not there. Not until I went to the churches of America and heard her pupils aflame with righteousness did I understand the secret of her genius and power. America is great because she is good and if America ever ceases to be good, America will cease to be great.

Alexis de Tocqueville

History is the essence of innumerable biographies.

Thomas Carlyle

Father says, "Your mother should really keep going to work. If she stays home, what will she do? Watch me watch television?"

Noah's Restaurant, father-son lunch

Slumber not in the tents of your fathers. The world is advancing, advance with it.

Grandfather John Adams Smith Brown,
advice to his grandson, the author, 1936

Old Charleston, South Carolina
Called a City but South of Broad, a Village
Fanny Kemble, an English actress on tour in 1838, visited Old Charleston, the oldest city she had seen in America. She wrote:

> *"The appearance ... is highly picturesque, a word which can apply to none of the other American towns."*

Charlestonians are proud, house proud, garden proud, and ever so willing to take pains to make their intimate environment near perfect.

For we must consider that we shall be a city set upon a hill.

John Winthrop

Winthrop was the first pilgrim of the Massachusetts Colony who established the base for the extraordinary survival of New England as a prelude to the United States of America.

If the American Revolution had produced nothing but the Declaration of Independence it would have been worthwhile.

Samuel Eliot Morrison

Machiavelli, in The Prince, *cautioned princes to be careful to commit cruelties only when absolutely necessary. (Sort of like, Don't beat a child in anger.)*

This is the way the world ends, not with a bang but a whimper.

T. S. Eliot

Civilization is a movement…and not a condition, a voyage and not a harbor.

> Arnold Toynbee

Every human being carries a record of his or her evolutionary past—going back to its beginning millions of years ago. All our root genealogy fades into the dawn of history.

Politics are almost as exciting as war, and quite as dangerous. In war you can only be killed once, but in politics many times.

> Winston Churchill

We came too late to say anything which has not been said already.

> Jean de La Bruyère

In the ancient poem, the *Aeneid*, poet Virgil tells a stunning story of the search for a home and the obligations people have to their parents and to their children: it does resonate with us, not least because the culture it springs from remains the bedrock of ours.

> Malcolm Jones

The history of this century teaches a grim truth: when at peace the nation should always assume that it may be living in what subsequent historians will call "interwar years."

> George F. Will

Few statesmen excel in stature and character more than Britain's great leader, Edmund Burke. During the American Revolution, Edmund Burke tended openly to support the infant American cause . . . My mentor and senior partner, R. Keith Kane, Esq., was a gifted leader and friend. He excelled at all endeavors. He died too early and left behind an extraordinary legacy of integrity, decency and honor. His widow, Amanda, kindly passed on to me with a gentle message volumes of The Works of Edmund Burke, *a most gratifying gift of his memory and his contribution to great leadership, law and order at a time before a sad decline in the integrity and strength of the American bar profession*

(See Rascals: The Decline of the American Law Profession (Benchmark Press, 1989)

Remember Hillary Clinton's star speech at her confirmation hearing as U.S. Secretary of State: "Foreign policy" she called "smart power," that we must use the full range of tools at our disposal—diplomatic, economic, military, political, legal and cultural...picking the right words or combination of words for each situation. Smart power, she surmises, will be the vanguard of our new foreign policy: "Recall the ancient poet of Rome, Terence, who declared that in every endeavor, the seemly course for wise men and women is to try persuasion first."

There is a limit at which forbearance ceases to be a virtue.

Edmund Burke

Who controls the past controls the future: Who controls the present controls the past.

George Orwell

President Barack Obama's Inaugural Address

(Selected Quote)

In reaffirming the greatness of our nation, we understand that greatness is never a given. It must be earned.

January 21st, 2009

WELL-BEING

Well-being is a gracious offshoot of happiness, but is not deemed happiness itself. Well-being encompasses a subtle variation of attitudes, charms, preferences, enthusiasms, successes. Basically, well-being is a highly tuned appreciation of those essential values and qualities that are available to most people without cost, stress, or bankruptcy, for example: well-being includes a cold beer on a hot night and a dry martini in inclement weather; observing a magnificent rainbow following a pouring rain; climbing a mountain in comfortable shoes; enjoying food in a favorite restaurant; learning your lost dog has been found; waking up anywhere *feeling good*; realizing as you go to work that you are living the good life, solvent, with the person you truly love and who loves you as well. Well-being is a gracious phenomenon that is available to most souls who are endowed with spirit-energy and discipline of heart. Also this goal encompasses an enviable attitude toward life itself, an attitude that can both transcend and inspire our lives for years to come, without suffering the baggage of poverty, abuse, illness, depression, and the major meltdown of boredom in any environment.

Attitude about life, opportunities, adventure, visiting friends and neighbors, nurturing a garden, taking time to enjoy a setting sun, the uplift of a morning sunrise—carpe diem—*seize the day!!*

Celebration is yet another form of human play.
                    Kay Redfield Jamison

Enthusiasm *is the* source of creativity, *from the Greek* entheos—*the god within each of us.*

You are a king by your own fireside, as much as any monarch in his throne.
                    Miguel de Cervantes

To mean well is nothing without to do well.
                    Plautus, 190 B.C.

The word *home* is derived from the Old Norse *heimr* and combines a description of place with psychological attributes, such as well-being, contentment, and sense of belonging, regarding the family as individuals and the home as a place of refuge.
                    Johnny Grey

In the midst of winter I finally learned that there was in me an invincible summer.
                    Albert Camus

First, be your own boss. Never retire or the brain deteriorates.

Harsh technological efficiency plays against civility—in the computer age we risk losing those qualities that comprise civilization.

Some of the most wonderful pleasures of civilized life come from small comforts.

Learned Hand, the quintessential jurist, wrote his best legal opinions in his seventies.

A garden may be said to be the aura of a house. Without it a country house or cottage lacks its right and proper atmosphere, and is left as bald as a small child's drawing.
> William Beach Thomas

Blessings come from care, troubles from carelessness.
> Buddha

Never leave your village when your garden is in bloom.
> Jack Lenor Larsen

Instead of concentrating on the seven deadly sins, think sometimes of the seven virtues: Faith, Hope, Charity, Prudence, Justice, Fortitude, and Temperance.

Common sense is not so common.

> Voltaire

Give me health and a day, and I will make the pomp of emperors ridiculous.

> Ralph Waldo Emerson

Gratitude is a fruit of great cultivation, you do not find it among gross people.

> Samuel Johnson

Each cigarette smoked takes 11 minutes off our life.

Health is the first muse and sleep is the condition to produce it.

> Ralph Waldo Emerson

All farewells should be sudden.

> Lord Byron

Come live with me, and be my love;
And we will all the pleasures prove
That valleys, groves, hills, and fields,
Woods or steepy mountain yields.

> Christopher Marlowe

Start somewhere in a corner and go from there.

> Frank Cabot, *Advice to Novice Gardeners*

Managing Illness

If there is a cure,

What good is discontent?

If there is no cure,

What good is discontent?

Shantideva, 8th century master

Consider in our inner journey the words of Shantideva:

As long as space endures,

…And as long as sentient beings exist,

May I, too, remain,

To dispel the misery of the world.

We often have an eating disorder because we eat disorderly.

The Warm Riches of Home

Wherever you are, whatever your place, create your space as you like it. When you go away, you carry it with you, and long for the return to the comfort, inspiration, and love of your own home.

What is hateful to you

Do not do to your neighbor.

That is the whole Torah.

The rest is commentary.

Hillel, 30 B.C.- A.D. 10, Torah spiritual leader

The movies and television have developed a pornography of violence far more demoralizing than the pornography of sex.
>Arthur Schlesinger, Jr.

Greed, violence, pornography and drugs are the four enemies of our fragile civilization.

Be careful of what you want; it has a way of turning up when and where one least expects it. Be sure you are strong enough to live with it when it happens.
>Michael Drury

An old Chinese saying describes the perfect spot to live: The water is clear, the trees are lush, the wind is mild, and the sun is bright. Small villages and large cities were founded in accordance with this principle for a place conducive to human habitation—a place with good feng shui will inevitably attract an increasing number of residents.

Yes, boredom is rage spread thin—the most insidious malady to slyly strike us down. Beware—as time sputters. Know you're off your path. Take action ASAP. Only you can restore your personal vitality and love of life.
The secret of well-being is simplicity.
>Peter Mathiesen

Of all calamities intemperance is the greatest.
> Thomas Jefferson

Opulence and freedom are mankind's two greatest blessings.
> Adam Smith

Chase perfection, and settle for excellence along the way.
> Vince Lombardi

Wine is of the earth. It has that vital force so it can stir our memory of things in life that we love.
> Jonathan Alsop

You should get all the fragrances you can!
> Young lady to her companion while smelling the roses at our picket fence in Stonington Village as they passed in front of the cottage on a summer evening

Gandhi taught us, if we practice an eye for an eye and a tooth for a tooth, soon the whole world will be blind and toothless.

Just as true humor is laughing at oneself, true humanity is knowledge of oneself—self-awareness makes human experience resonant!
> Alan Watts

Dr. Samuel Johnson believed most of our follies of life stem from our attempt to be someone other than ourselves.

Each spring when we garden, or watch new grass come up, there is the same secret promise of hope.

> Mac Griswold, Pleasures of the Garden

Be calm in arguing.

> George Herbert

Resentment is the pathway to anger, depression, and unhappiness. Author Malachy McCourt likens resentment to taking poison and waiting for the other person to die.

Lawrence Durrell, the novelist, observed that each one of us has a home landscape, the place we return to in our mind's eye when we contemplate our beginnings.

When a person does not display any body language at all, you can be assured that passivity is the body language.

Everybody today seems to be in such a terrible rush, anxious for greater developments and greater riches so that children have very little time with their parents. Parents have very little time for each other, and in the home begins the disruption of the peace of the world.

> Mother Teresa

Health in Our Genes?

Stress, anxiety, depression: the new science of evolutionary psychology finds the roots of modern maladies in our genes.

Time Magazine

A breathless statistic: Our heart beats three billion times in an average lifetime.

Of all the sad words of tongue or pen, the saddest are these: "It might have been."

J. G. Whittier

Thomas Jefferson esteemed the twin qualities of light and air, especially desirable when confined to hot sultry periods in Philadelphia (1775-1776) as a delegate to the Continental Congress. He would escape to the countryside to breathe and enjoy rural light and pure air, the benefits there of the good life. He spoke of this benefit many times.

A G E

The Indignities of Old Age

Barrister John Mortimer was an active writer and devastating wit in England up to the day of his death at eighty-five. He had created the entertaining character Rumpole, and delighted Alexandra and me at lively parties with smashing anecdotes and memorable stories about his life experiences—some of them true. . . .

Mortimer seemed to have a firm fixation on the sad process of ageing, especially when reading to us a script of his own obituary…suggesting it might be "great fun" as he read it aloud to a cast of listeners! "Dying is a matter of slapstick and pratfalls," he wrote, in *The Summer of a Dormouse: A Year of Growing Old Disgracefully*. Mortimer continued, "The ageing process is not gradual or gentle. It rushes up, pushes you over and runs off laughing. No one should grow old who isn't ready to appear ridiculous," he said, smiling.

Today I learned I'd lost the happiness and wisdom of a good friend.

January 17ᵗʰ, 2009

Old age is an incurable disease.
> Seneca

Grace in old age smoothes the way: the key is simply graciousness in all things.

To me, old age is always fifteen years older than I am.
> Bernard Baruch

A total makeover is not possible after forty.
> Maureen Dowd

Old age is not such an uncomfortable thing, if one gives one's self up to it with good grace.
> Horace Walpole,
> letter to the Countess of Ailesbury, 1774

To many a youth,
And many a maid
Dancing in the checkered shade.
And young and old
Come forth to play
On a sunshine afternoon.
> John Milton

It takes a long time to become young.
> Pablo Picasso

In spite of illness, in spite even of the archenemy sorrows, one can remain alive long past the usual date of disintegration if one is unafraid of change, insatiable in intellectual curiosity, interested in big things, and happy in small ways.

Edith Wharton

The essence of age is intellect.

Ralph Waldo Emerson

When you reach September
Oh, the days dwindle down
To a precious few…
And these few precious days
I'll spend with you.

Maxwell Anderson

Try to avoid dementia by daily activity; curiosity; increased, diverse vocabulary; and especially love, until the very end, while maintaining at all cost your innate spirit-energy.

The trick is to grow up without getting old.

Frank Lloyd Wright

"People don't grow old. When they stop growing, they become old." This is what an eighty-year-old patient told Dr. Deepak Chopra.

Education is the best provision for old age.

        Aristotle

Old age isn't so bad when you consider the alternative.

        Whitney North Seymour, Jr., Esq.

The whole of life is a journey toward youthful old age, the most gratifying time of our lives—a harvest time when the riches of life are reaped and enjoyed, yet a special period for self-development and expansion.

        Ashley Montagu

He who is calm and of a happy nature will hardly feel the pressure of age, but to him of the opposite disposition, youth and age are equally burdensome.

        Plato

Legendary Greek playwright Euripides said if we could be twice young and twice old we could correct all our mistakes.

I'm not young enough to know everything.

        J. M. Barrie

As we grow older we experience the growth of our innate spirituality and the diminishment of our physical strength. In many ways, we can become a better person.

I am not old. I have just lived a long time.

George Ballantine

Relax: science reports to us that there are now no effective anti-ageing medicines.

It is better to wear out than to rust out.

Bishop Richard Cumberland (1631-1718)

H O N O R

Abraham Lincoln
1809-1865
200th birthday: February 12th, 2009

Born in a log cabin in the backwoods of Kentucky, Lincoln taught himself, reading and rereading a small stock of books, a rawboned young man of strength and character as well as much popularity among the inhabitants of the frontier town. Early on, he exhibited a flair for storytelling. His sincerity and capability won respect that was further enhanced by his ability to hold his own in the roughest society.

In 1836 he obtained his license as an attorney. Lincoln displayed great ability in law, a ready grasp of argument, and sincerity, lucidity, and color. In this new element, Lincoln soon blossomed into a major figure in local, then national, politics. He honed his speaking skills in seven debates with his rival, Stephen A. Douglas. Abraham Lincoln was on his way to immortality.

On the night of April 14th, 1865, when attending a performance at Ford's Theater, he was shot by the actor John Wilkes
Booth. The next morning, Lincoln died. His death was an occasion for grief even among those who had been his opponents, and
many considered him a martyr. As time passed he became more
and more the object of adulation; a "Lincoln Legend" appeared.
Yet even if his faults and mistakes are acknowledged, he stands
out as a statesman of noble vision, great humanity, and remarkable political skill. Lincoln was a good man and dearly loved by
those who had the good fortune to know him.

There are higher qualities than competence. The rarest and
highest is honor—a commodity in the shortest supply.

Murray Kempton

*Murray Kempton was a New York reporter who sought news
on a bicycle. He is renowned for his indefatigable honor and
fairness.*

What is left when honor is lost?

Publius Syrus

You can tell the character of every man when you see how he
receives praise.

Seneca

He who says there is no such thing as an honest man, you may be
sure is himself a knave.

George Berkeley

The louder he talked of his honor, the faster we counted our spoons.
Ralph Waldo Emerson

*Winston Churchill recognized early on in his extraordinary life
of adventure and achievement that from the highest to the
humblest tasks, all are of equal honor, and all do have their
part to play. Yet in today's world of turmoil and terror there
seems to be among all classes a reluctance to speak out about
the country's need for honor, openly expressed and openly
achieved.*

*Abraham Lincoln is a case in point: in a speech at
Edwardsville, Illinois on September 11, 1858, Lincoln gave
meaning, honor and purpose to the Civil War that speaks to
us still. What constitutes the bulwark of our own liberty and
independence? "Our reliance," he said, "is on the love of liberty which God has planted in our bosoms." It's significant,
perhaps, that Lincoln spoke these few penetrating words on a
date similar to one bound with infamy.*

*Questions of honesty are raised as much by appearances as
by reality in politics. Because they invite public distrust, they
need to be addressed no less directly than we would address
evidence of expressly illegal corruption. Anyone engaging
in public affairs should be aware that the appearance of
impropriety or corruption can be as deadly to reputation as
proven crime.*

Honor insists on modesty, to which it is firmly bound.

The Conduct of Life, 1860

Rudyard Kipling said that he celebrated six honest men who taught him all he knew: their names were what, *and* why, *and* when, *and* how, *and* where, *and* who.
All you need to know to get started.

We cannot live our dreams. We are lucky enough if we can give a sample of our best, and if in our hearts we can feel that it has been nobly done.

Justice Oliver Wendell Holmes, Jr.

Define wisdom as the application of truth and honesty to everyday life.

Let it be said that I am right rather than consistent.

John Marshall Harlan, Sr., grandfather of John Marshall Harlan, who himself attained the honor of appointment to the United States Supreme Court

A man should go where he won't be tempted.

Sir Thomas More

MEMORY

It is certainly nice to remember that our memories alone can enrich our lives. We can stimulate these memories of the past, laced as they are with vivid anecdotes and colorful stories of life's curious ironies and adventures. We can actually capture and retrieve the best of these memories—so we are able to run them in our own minds, at will, like video film at less cost and bother...

The message here is to live triumphantly and record these private thoughts for yourself, your family, your friends, and above all, for all time. Cicero, as early as 80 B.C., reminds us that memory is the treasury and guardian of all things.

Scientists have discovered that when we become more mature we begin to experience a greater faculty to recall—sometimes in startling detail—events, places, people, conversations, colors, smells, and narratives we thought had long ago been buried in the past.

Excerpts from *Flights of Memory, Days Before Yesterday*: A Memoir, with a foreword by Alexandra Stoddard

Winston Churchill rose up to make his maiden speech in the House of Commons. Suddenly he lost his memory of what he was then to say...humiliated, he stepped down in the hushed chamber. After this unhappy event, Winston Churchill from then on invariably placed his notes before him.

In a time of deep crises financial and social, wars, illness and such distress as the Great Depression, with its current recurrence in 2007-9, and unhappily onward, can we remember when Jimmy Stewart played in Frank Capra's 1939 movie classic, Mr. Smith Goes to Washington:
(Arriving, excited, at Lincoln's masterful Memorial in Washington D.C., near the Potomac River): That Lincoln Memorial—gee whiz! Mr. Lincoln, there he is, looking straight at you as you come up the steps, like he was waiting for somebody to come along!

Once a caterpillar becomes a butterfly, it doesn't remember being a caterpillar; it briefly remembers being a little butterfly.

George Vaillant

Sharpening Your Recall

The one who thinks over his experiences most, and weaves them into systematic relations with each other, will be the one with the best memory.

Association of the mind with some thing or person is the best way to remember a name, which is often of importance in social relationships.

Memories are lanterns at the back of the ship. Memories are our treasure, enhancing and enriching our lives. Recall at will the ecstasy of re-experiencing our life and our love.

ECONOMICS

"We have involved ourselves in a colossal muddle, having blundered in the control of a delicate machine, the working of which we do not understand."

So wrote the bright economic iconoclast John Maynard Keynes, in the great slump of the 1930s. Thirteen months had passed since the crash of 1929. The world was living, in Keynes's words, in the shadow of one of the greatest economic catastrophes of modern history.

The sixteenth-century psychic Nostradamus predicted the termination of the world commencing in the summer of 1999. In two dreadful unexpected periods many people suspected the termination of our world as we know it: the Great Depression of 1929-37, and a dire economic recession in 2007-10.

Sumptuary Code: A Cesspool

1. Auto executives out of Detroit using private jets for lobbying trips to Washington D.C.
2. John Thain, who was humiliated because it is no longer acceptable to spend $35,000 on a commode for a Merrill Lynch washroom

3. Wall Street executives giving out the same sort of bo-nuses they've been giving out for years

4. Tom Daschle, who accepted a quick five million dollars in fees off his Senate prestige

5. Rich people who now suffer similar self-immolation be-cause they don't understand that the rules of privileged society have undergone a radical transformation—too used to setting their own norms

6. Now the norms of acceptable behavior are set not by the former privileged class but rather by those who presum-ably live in Ward Three—a section of northwest Wash-ington, D.C. where many Democratic staffers, regulators, journalists, lawyers, Obama aides and senior civil ser-vants live, who now run the banks and many major indus-tries. For some reason these rich people are disliked by the less privileged neighbors who choose to engage them-selves in unacknowledged self-pity...

7. As David Brooks says in his *New York Times* column of February 3rd, 2009, sometimes with tongue in cheek, What we must realize, above all, is the rich no longer control this economy and its mores. Ward Three people do, and their rule has just begun.

The cost of a thing...is the amount of life it requires to be exchanged for it, immediately or in the long run.

Henry David Thoreau

Taxes

The wise jurist Learned Hand put it well: There is nothing sinister in so arranging one's affairs as to keep taxes as low as possible. Everybody does so, rich or poor; and all do right, for nobody owes any public duty to pay more than the law demands; taxes are enforced extractions, not voluntary contributions. To demand more in the name of morals is mere cant.

A compliment is the only thing you pay that costs nothing; given freely, it is priceless, a Zen riddle of civilized existence.

S. S. Fair

Brooke Astor, delightful aristocrat and philanthropist, died at 105 in 2007. With a wink and a smile, she would sometimes quote Dolly Levi in Thornton Wilder's play The Matchmaker: *"Money is like manure, it's not worth a thing unless it's spread around."*

Economics is a nice way to keep economists employed.

John Kenneth Galbraith

George H. W. Bush once called supply-side economics "voodoo."

Desire for wealth can never be satisfied. Those who possess it are excited by the wish to have some more, and yet more.

Cicero

He who is contented is rich.

Lao-Tzu

We live in a world of inequality and diversity...Now the big challenge and threat is the gap in wealth and health that separates rich and poor...Here is the greatest single problem and danger facing the world of the third millennium.

David S. Landes

Riches don't alleviate, only change, one's troubles.

Epicurus

Where there is money, there is fighting.

Marian Anderson

Arriving at one goal is the starting point of another.

John Dewey

Economics 101

Economists are right when they say that zero is an infinitely smaller number than one. Multiply by a billion and you still have zero.

Joel Achenbach

Everything is worth what its purchasers will pay for it.

Publius Syrus, 1st century B.C.

Still the rule.

To give away money is an easy matter and in any man's power. But to decide when to give it, and how large and when, and for what purpose and how, is neither in every man's power nor an easy matter.

Aristotle

You can't make someone else's choices. You shouldn't let someone else make yours.

Colin Powell

None of us really understands what's going on with all these numbers.

David Stockman, former Budget Director, describing supply-side economics

He is only rich who owns the day. There is no king, rich man, fairy, or demon who possesses such power as that.

Ralph Waldo Emerson

Every swindle is driven by a desire for easy money. It's the one thing the swindler and the swindled have in common.

Mitchell Zuckoff

I keep thinking of Bernard Madoff.

Superfluous wealth can buy superfluities only. Money is not required to buy one necessity of the soul.

Henry David Thoreau

Too much money makes people stupid, dull, unseeing and uninteresting. Be careful.

> Abby Aldrich Rockefeller, advising her young second son, Nelson Rockefeller. Abby's advice left Nelson wondering all his life what was too much money, so he settled for romance.

Among the lessons of Jack Kerouac's novel and initial scroll On the Road, *John Leland tells us, is this pithy interpretive advice*: "Low overhead and a sense of improvisation make for a good life."

Verify, verify the quick and easy deal offered to you.

Avoid—carefully—being the guarantor of someone else's debt.

We spend half our lives engaged in the discipline of learning. We spend the rest of our lives unlearning what we learned. (The hard part is the unlearning that should lead to enlightenment.)

The generality of mankind are contented to be estimated by what they possess instead of what they are.

> William Hazlitt

Pleasure is only the shadow of Happiness.

> Hindu proverb

CHARACTER

On Martin Luther King Day I was drawn to look into what his exact words were in his famed speech on civil rights in June 1963—now called his "Dream Speech":

> I have a dream this afternoon that my four little children, [repeating] that my four little children, will not come up in the same young days I came up within, but will be judged on the basis of the content of their character, and not the color of their skin.

I remain moved by these eloquent words spoken by Martin Luther King Jr., who intelligently chose to emphasize character as the distinctive quality of one person over another. This attribute is often overlooked in the rush to name wealth and power and self-importance as the virtues worthy of our attention…Character is rightly revealed as an ethical and moral strength.

Heraclitus taught in ancient days that a man or woman's character is their fate. Now we recognize that fate and character are simply the very same conception—just as the road up and down are one and the same. Plato assured us long ago that nothing endures but change. But only character stands out as the supreme attribute necessary for happiness and love.

In the Arena

The credit belongs to the man who is actually in the arena; whose face is marred by dust and sweat and blood; who strives valiantly; who errs and comes short again and again; who knows the great enthusiasm, the great devotions, and spends himself in a worthy cause; who, at the best, knows in the end the triumph of high achievement; and who, at the worst, if he fails, at least fails while daring greatly, so that his place shall never be with those cold and timid souls who know neither victory nor defeat.

Theodore Roosevelt

Life is like riding a bicycle: you don't fall off unless you stop pedaling.

Claude Pepper

Obituary: J. E. Lumbard

Lumbard—J. Edward. On June 3, 1999. All the lawyers who served with him when he was United States Attorney for the Southern District of New York, and whom he referred to as partners, mourn the passing of a great lawyer, a fine teacher, an outstanding United States Attorney and a brilliant Chief Judge of the Court of Appeals for the Second Circuit. It was a privilege to have served with him.

The Lumbard Association

Courage is the first of human qualities because it is the quality which guarantees all others.

Winston Churchill

Dealing with courtesy, kindness, courage, intimacy—there are few who have exhibited consistently the four pillars of good character.

Well done is better than well said.

Benjamin Franklin

Benjamin Franklin—the ultimate one-sentence evisceration about John Adams: "Always an honest man, often a wise one, but sometimes, and in some things, absolutely out of his senses."

A thought is often original, though you have uttered it a hundred times.

Oliver Wendell Holmes, Sr.

Motto Engraved on the Coins of Hadrian

Libertas, Humanitas, Felicitas

Liberty, Humanity, and Grace

The Roman Emperor Hadrian was succeeded by Marcus Aurelius.

Three may keep a secret, if two of them are dead.

Benjamin Franklin

Each decision you make is a destiny decision. Each choice is a destiny choice. Character is the key to happiness.

Character above all determines our fate.

The last of human freedoms—to choose one's attitude in any given set of circumstances, to choose one's own way.
Viktor Frankl

Everyone largely reacts in the way they physically and mentally feel, the feel permeates the behavior. So understood—we study the person and his conduct. Character is conduct, Henry James said, and then, conduct is character.

The "cover up" usually doubles the scandal and creates the implosion of real harm. Prime example: Richard Nixon and Watergate.

Perhaps the most vital and enduring intuition we can acquire is a profound understanding of human nature.

Man is not the creature of circumstances. Circumstances are the creatures of men.
Benjamin Disraeli

The greater man the greater courtesy.
Alfred Lord Tennyson

Never give in! Never give in! Never, never, never, never—
> Winston Churchill

Winston Churchill's sense of humor saved his political life—and granted him immortality.

Loyalty is perhaps the only absolute virtue.
> George F. Kennan

George F. Kennan, when U.S. Ambassador to the Soviet Union, wrote the famous longest telegram to the State Department, defining with clarity the nature and complexity of the Cold War. He served our public interests with brilliance. He was a superior, honorable public servant, had a marvelous personality and a high reputation internationally for honor and wisdom.

The imprints of childhood are the strongest and most enduring stamp of personality.
> George F. Kennan

Thought which does not ultimately guide action is incomplete.
> John Dewey

Action that does not lead to reflection is more gravely incomplete.
> Lewis Mumford

The inner life is stronger than the outer norms.
> Jacques Barzun

Nothing on earth consumes a man more quickly than the passion of resentment.

> Friedrich Nietzsche

The pretense of knowledge where there is none is fraud.

> U.S. Supreme Court Justice
> Benjamin N. Cardozo

It is not so important what we say, it is important what we do.

> Bishop T. D. Jakes, at a prayer service for victims of Hurricane Katrina at the Washington Cathedral, September 16th, 2005

When sometimes you are feeling superior—yes, elite, and insufferably smug just remember that we human beings share almost all of our genes with chimpanzees, 88% of them with rodents and 60% with chickens.

> The Economist

These statistics may be right, although the message is humbling.

It is a great ability to be able to conceal one's ability.

> Virgil

Character is, by itself, invisible wealth.

I think the necessity of being ready increases. Look to it.

> Abraham Lincoln

If you want to find a rainbow you have to stand some rain.

You know that the *beginning* is the most important part of any work, especially in the case of a young and tender thing;—for that is the time *character* is being formed and the desired impression is more readily taken.

Plato, *The Republic*

Two movie moguls were having breakfast at the Beverly Hills Hotel poolside. The first said, "Damn it, you're lying to me!" The other replied, "Yes, I know, you're right. But hear me out!"

Personality being a word whose Latin root means musk.

A courageous effort consecrates an unhappy mind.

Lewis Mumford

Class can be defined as the ability in any situation to be yourself.

Henry Lowell Madden

Often it's the unspoken that guides the spoken.

Jay Iselin

Fear follows crime, and is its punishment.

Voltaire

Voltaire—a genius—lived a good life of sublime intuition.

I have only a second-rate brain but I think I have a capacity for action.
> Franklin Delano Roosevelt,
> first inaugural address, March 4th, 1933

I cannot cause any improvement in anyone except with the help of
the goodness and kindness which already is inherent in this person.
> Immanuel Kant

You can't step twice in the same river.
> Plato

All is flux, nothing stops still.
> Heraclitus

Popularity? It is glory's small change.
> Victor Hugo

The secret of joy in work is contained in one word: *excellence*.
To know how to do something well is to enjoy it.
> Anatole Broyard

Excellence is the standard.

Character is higher than intellect.
> Ralph Waldo Emerson

Character is perseverance; perseverance is character.
Character is destiny—and paramount.

ART

I often think of art as food for the soul. We hunger for it, dream about it, try to create it ourselves, mostly indulge in its imaginative creativity, especially in bold colors, impregnated with light.

Art goes along with the artist in our mind. Our favorite artist is Roger Mühl, an Alsatian genius of enormous talent, energy and constraint. He lived happily in the high beauty of Mougins, France, in Provence, until his untimely death on April 4th, 2008. Roger Mühl for many years was a true friend of our family. Alexandra devotedly collected his artwork from the time he arrived in the United States for his first visit in the 1960s. Like the most perfect beauty of the Greeks of the fifth century A.D., Roger Mühl's paintings virtually every day was the pure and unadorned. His color palette was magnificent, fresh, and filled with light drawn from the skies of Provence overlooking the Maritime Alps and the Mediterranean Sea.

We will never forget the warm friendship and character of Roger Mühl and his wife Line, and the magnanimous art he created in his noble lifetime.

*When we visit the art museums we overhear people comment-
ing snidely, "Why, a child of mine could paint something like
that," pointing to an array of paintings by Pablo Picasso. Yet
above the fray, Picasso forthrightly asserts that his "lifelong
ambition is to paint like a child."*

A work of art is never finished, only abandoned.
                                    Anatole France

*Quoted by Edmund Morris, responding to criticism that he's
taking over thirteen years to complete his biography of former
president Ronald Reagan.*

Criticism is easy, art is difficult.
                                    Phillipe Néricault Restouches

*What the architect Sir Christopher Wren's tomb says of the
cathedral built over it:*
Si monumentum requires, circumspice.
"If you seek his monument, look around you."

My painting is not important. The important thing is keeping busy.
                                    Grandma Moses (Anna Mary Robertson),
                                    in 1954, when she was ninety-four years old
*Grandma Moses was then wise enough to know the key im-
portance of living well: Keep busy and celebrate life.*

Tea, like the arts, challenges and consoles us, enlivens our days and lifts our spirits.

There is no intellectual or emotional substitute for the authentic, the original, the unique masterpiece.
    Paul Mellon

Since the beginning of the nineteenth century, art has been defined again and again by its devotees as the highest spiritual expression of man.

Art is the transforming experience.
    Joseph Campbell

Just to paint is great fun. The colors are lovely to look at and delicious to squeeze out. Matching them, however crudely, with what you see is fascination and absolutely absorbing. Try it if you have not done so—before you die!
    Winston Churchill

The future of art is in light.
    Henri Matisse

Art is unthinkable without risk and spiritual self-sacrifice.
    Boris Pasternak

Just as there is no substitute for original works of art, there is no substitute for the world of direct sensual experience.

Taste is not content with seeing, with knowing the beauty of a work; it has to feel it, to be touched by it.
> Voltaire

I want to reach that state of condensation of sensation which constitutes a picture.
> Henri Matisse (1869-1954)

Georges Clemenceau, France's World War I Premier was one of Claude Monet's dearest friends. When Monet died in December 1926, Clemenceau came quickly to say farewell. He found Monet's coffin covered with the traditional black pall. Clemenceau tore it off immediately and seized a bright multi-colored shawl to drape over the coffin, saying, "*Pas de noir pour Monet*" ("No black for Monet.")

In a career of less than 20 years, Toulouse-Lautrec was our artistic genius of explosive production—737 canvasses, 275 watercolors, 363 prints and posters, 5084 drawings, 300 pornographic works. He died at thirty-six… possibly from exhaustion.

The most perfect beauty, to the Greeks of the fifth century A.D., was the *pure* and *unadorned*.
> Nicholas Gates

Cézanne visited Giverny in the fall of 1894. He viewed the incipient water garden and the Clos Normand and then examined Claude Monet's latest paintings. Cézanne was not an ebullient man, but at that moment he was heard to exclaim: "Monet is but an eye...but good God, what an eye!"

EDUCATION

My "education" began when I was living with a loving family in New York City, arriving in 1927 at five years old at the time Lindbergh flew in May to Paris; as a fourth child I felt cosseted and secure despite the regular lecture by my parents in the library about the Great Depression with endless talks about cutting back all—or most—expenses and childhood privileges of happy times, toys, clothes that were not just handed down by my brother George. My next so-called education was being sent to a local city school where I was relatively free of hectoring by my siblings, who characterized me as "the baby;" excluded from all their parties, celebrations, and conversations, I was an unfortunate outsider.

My next education came to me one day when my father began to notice his youngest child. He had a seat on the Stock Exchange where he seldom sat. Unemployed in the early thirties, he would come home to our apartment at 1172 Park Avenue with little if anything to do. He would retire to the little library, become lonely and then bring me in for a talk. The subject was the then desperate financial collapse all around us. My father was clear and even persuasive in explaining the causes of the Great Depression and what the future might entail…

I was first enrolled at a school nearby that, to my dismay, turned out to be essentially a girls' school with a somewhat scary woman as headmistress. I begged my father to send me instead to the Browning School for boys, which he finally agreed to do. This unexpected development constituted my continuing education, providing great joy for years to come, until, following my brother, I was sent to St. Andrews boarding school in Middletown, Delaware, that lit up my life enormously. The headmaster, Walden Pell, and the able faculty created an environment that made students' lives a great pleasure, and a marvelous sports program.

After graduation from St. Andrews School I was luckily granted admission to Yale College, class of 1944. This new scholastic event was, for me, a wonderful uplifting educational experience. The Japanese attack on Pearl Harbor cut short our freshman year. Three years in the U.S. Army soon followed, that I must confess was educational as well as strengthening my writing and reading. In 1948, to my surprise, I was admitted to the Yale Law School, where Dean DeVane gave me full academic credit for work during the war at the University of California, sufficient to obtain a doctorate in law. This was a step toward real education.

This boost led to being hired by a New York City law firm Senior Litigator—John Marshall Harlan, who became my mentor—as an associate, leading to assignment as his Assistant Counsel on the New York State Crime Commission. A few years later

Judge J. Edward Lumbard, United States Attorney, hired me as a prosecutor of organized crime. Mr. Harlan, in the meantime, was appointed by Governor Thomas E. Dewey to be a Justice of the United States Supreme Court.

In 2007 the Yale Law School selected 303 bound volumes of my principal lawsuits over fifty years of practice in the U.S. Supreme Court and Appellate Courts for its collection, now available for the use of students and scholars and located in the Manuscripts and Archives section of the Yale University Law Library. I am deeply grateful to those lawyers, judges and mentors who provided this training and encouraged my work over half a century. These years gave me a form of learning and fulfillment I will never forget and will appreciate for all time.

The rich life is a life of learning.

Education should be of achievements, each raising the individual to a higher level of awareness, understanding, and growing knowledge.

The strongest principle of growth lies in human choice.
>   George Eliot

A curious traveler asked poet William Wordsworth's servant to show him her master's study. She answered: "Here is his library, but his study is out of doors."
>   Henry David Thoreau

Letter to the Editor

In an intelligent letter to the editor of the New York Times, *Brad Bradford made two good points:*

1) *The ultimate value of a college degree may not be the university's status but the knowledge a student acquired.*

2) *That, he said, includes the ability to* think critically and ask pertinent questions, *the confidence to form an opinion, knowing that new information might change an opinion, and the* aptitude to teach oneself after graduation.

If one is bent upon observation, nothing…is trivial.

Henry James

People compose new knowledge by mentally playing out combinatorial interactions in their mind's eye.

Steven Pinker

Thinkers are gifted with the innate ability to wander and wonder through various options in their minds until arriving at a satisfactory resolution.

Encouragement, not criticism, is the great educator.

Everyone is ignorant except on certain subjects.

Mark Twain

Personally I am always ready to learn, although I do not always like being taught.

Winston Churchill

Imitation is the slow way to learning.

Faithful study of the liberal arts humanizes character and permits it not to be cruel.

Ovid

Everyone has an opinion, but some people shouldn't.

Michael Kinsley

A learned blockhead is a greater blockhead than an ignorant one.

Benjamin Franklin

The greatest pain is boredom; the finest pleasure is curiosity satisfied. Boredom and pleasure are the flip sides of the coin.

Curiosity is one of the permanent and certain characteristics of a vigorous mind.

Samuel Johnson

The direction in which education starts a man will determine his future life.

Plato

FRIENDSHIP

Our culture relies on wit and wisdom of the past and present (as we are told by Fred R. Shapiro, lecturer in legal research at the Yale Law School, New Haven, Connecticut), a true culture that leads to friendship, truth, and happiness.

Without friends no one would choose to live, though he had all other goods.

> Aristotle

Vote now for the greatest comforts: good and old friends.

Prosperity makes friends, adversity tries them.

> Publius Syrus

This maxim has stood up well, since the first century B.C.

Osborne Elliot died in 2008 after a long and courageous battle against cancer. I first met my new friend Oz when we became students in the 1930s at the Browning School on 62nd Street in

New York City. We both wore knickers and somehow believed we knew what was going on…

Oz was a whiz at words and phrases, so that over the years he grew as one of the most distinguished journalists. He rose to be editor in chief of Newsweek, where he started revamping the news magazine to become a strong rival to Time magazine. Oz introduced an exceptionally fine outlook on how and why his magazine should present to its readers a superb insight into those critical essential issues so needed to bring the United States into the new millennium of social and political maturity.

Oz and his wife Inger lived across the street from our cottage in Stonington Village, Connecticut, allowing us to sustain our friendship for many years. Few colleagues contributed so much to our community and society. With great admiration we salute Oz; appreciation of his memory and friendship will stay with us always.

Scientific researchers have recently been looking into some of the esoteric nature of friendship. Their studies indicate that there may be reason to suspect that genes do affect the friends we acquire. The subject itself somehow seems to interest most people despite the uncertainty and even ambiguity of our reasons for our friends becoming or remaining friends in the first place.

"Given that social networks of friends play important roles in determining a wide variety of things ranging from employment to wages to the spread of disease, it is important to understand why networks exhibit the patterns that they do," Matthew Jackson, a Stanford University economist, wrote for the study. The most recent study seems to indicate that "networks of friends also affect the spread of ideas and innovation, and there is a study suggesting that an individual's happiness depends on the happiness of others in his or her social network." So much for friends…

Of all the blessings bestowed on man and woman, few can match the comfort and loyalty of friendship. This is particularly true of friendships that go back a long way, through good times, and bad, misunderstandings and happy days together. Maintaining a friendship takes time, energy, and resolve. A sincere and happy visit can enliven a fading friendship with recalled anecdotes of earlier days together at school, college, adventurous trips, remembrances of your erstwhile friends' achievements that may light up a spark of reunion. Refreshing communication leads to solidifying a waning friendship. A good, newsy letter from you can work its magic—better than a quick phone call that may suggest that you want something given back rather than simply renewal of a friendship. Mark Twain spoke with a twinkle of the possibility of a sweet, steady, enduring friendship through a whole lifetime;—*if not asked to lend money…*

Conversation…is the art of never being a bore, of knowing how to say everything interestingly, to entertain no matter what, to be charming with nothing at all.

Guy de Maupassant

Intimates are predestined.

Henry Brooks Adams

If a man does not make new acquaintances as he advances through life, he will soon find himself left alone. A man, sir, should keep his friendship in a constant repair.

Samuel Johnson

To let friendship die away by negligence and silence is certainly not wise. It is to voluntarily throw away one of the greatest comforts.

A well-trained mind is the result of application, not inborn genius.

A lack of tact may betray a friendship, but too much tact may betray the truth.

Kay Redfield Jamison

The endearing elegance of female friendship.

Samuel Johnson

I am a part of all that I have met.

Alfred, Lord Tennyson

Kindness ultimately is to go the extra mile.

Be courteous to all but intimate with few, and let those few be well tried before you give them your confidence.

George Washington

A flatterer is a friend who is your inferior, or pretends to be so.
> Aristotle

Friendship makes our lives fulfilled.

Remember most friendships start with a compliment.

Abraham Lincoln understood that his nemesis could be extinguished by making him his friend.

I'm convinced that we can almost never know the precise motives of someone else, even old friends.
> Calvin Trillin

After three days men grow weary, of a wench, a guest, and rainy weather.
> Benjamin Franklin

Whom You Know

Osborne Elliot at a college commencement spoke candidly to the student body about what they would face after graduation: "Always remember," he said, "that it is not *who* you know…but *whom* you know."

SPIRITUALITY

The Serenity Prayer

For many years I have admired and followed the thoughtful words of Reverend Reinhold Niebuhr, who died in 1971, a superhuman being and exceptionally fine American theologian. He was especially renowned and much appreciated for his conviction that Christianity is obligated to confront directly ethical, social, and moral problems. His own profound and eloquent works include *The Nature and Destiny of Man* (1941-1943), and *Faith and History* (1949).

On August 2nd, 1942 the *New York Times* appeared to quote the "Serenity Prayer," in various forms set forth below, which, while wildly famous and repeatedly quoted, is now unfortunately acknowledged to be of uncertain origin and surrounded with misinformation. The first quotation in the *New York Times* in which these familiar words were published has caused an ambiguous stir ever since: "O God and Heavenly Father: Grant to us the serenity of mind to accept that which cannot be changed; the courage to change that which can be changed and the wisdom to know the one from the other."

209

In the July 12th, 1942 issue of the *New York Times* a corre-spondent of the "Queries and Answers" column asked for the origin of "Give me the patience to accept those things which I cannot change, the courage to change those things which can be changed and the wisdom to know the difference." On August 2nd, 1942, in response to that query, the text above was printed "clipped from a publication the name of which is not recalled" (sic) and another respondent attributed it to Niebuhr [first name Reinhold].

Alcoholics Anonymous, which has used the prayer very promi-nently, has given several conflicting accounts in its literature over the years, stating that it was found in an obituary in the *New York Times* or the *New York Herald Tribune* in 1939 or 1941, but the compiler of this observation has been unable to verify this in the relevant newspapers. . . . Others have attributed the Serenity Prayer to an eighteenth century German theologian name Oetinger, but this claim has been shown to be a misunderstanding.

Benjamin Franklin's favorite part of the Bible in the book of Kings: "An angel appeared to the boy Solomon and asked him, 'What gift do you want to rule your country? Riches?' Solomon replied, 'No, I choose understanding.'"

We often know something works before we know why.

> Dr. Larry Dossey, Santa Fe internist and author of *Healing Words*, in a comment on answered prayers

Ralph Waldo Emerson responded to Sampson Reed, who had argued one day that "it is not so in your experience, but is so in the other world." Emerson shot back: "Other world? There is no other world!" The debate goes on: Aristotle insisted our Earth was our only home, in contradiction of his mentor, Plato, who would point upward to the heavens while Aristotle pointedly indicated the earth below.

Humor is the vestibule of faith.
> Reinhold Niebuhr

If you seek the power before service, you'll neither get power, nor serve; if you seek to serve people more than to gain power, you will not only serve people, you will gain influence.
> Rev. Timothy J. Keller

We must be the change we wish to see in the world.
> Gandhi

To whom much is given, much is expected.
> Saint Luke

To each one of us grace has been given…
> Ephesians 4:7

"Grace" means "gift from God."

From lightning and tempest; from plague, pestilence and famine; from battle and murder, and from sudden death, Good
Lord, deliver us.

The Book of Common Prayer

Blaise Pascal, the 17th-century philosopher, invented a defini-
tion of God as "a circle whose center is everywhere and whose
circumference is nowhere."

Darwin Acknowledged a Creator?

Few environmentalists today mention that Charles Darwin,
in his famed book, On the Origin of Species (*1859*), *speaks*
approvingly of the second powers of life "originally breathed
by the Creator" and "from so simple a beginning endless
forms most beautiful and most wonderful have been and are
being 'evolved.'"

   In the last chapter of Darwin's The Descent of Man *he*
slyly inserts in 1871 the single most provocative remark one
can find anywhere: "We thus learn that man is descended
from a hairy quadruped, furnished with a tail and pointed
ears, probably arboreal in its habits, and an inhabitant of the
Old World."

The cosmos and human consciousness are infinite and there can
be no end to their exploration.

Jacques Barzun

A psalm implies serenity of soul, it is the author of peace which calms bewildering and seething thoughts. A psalm is a city of refuge from the demons, a means of inducing help from the angels, a weapon in fears by night, a rest from toils by day, a safeguard for infants, adornment for those at the height of their vigor, a consolation for the elders.

Human intuition and insight cannot be reduced to any set of rules.

> Roger Penrose, *Shadows of the Mind: A Search for the Missing Science of Consciousness* (Oxford University Press, 1994)

Your spirit animates with responsibility.

> General George S. Patton

O Lord, support us all the day long, until the shadows lengthen and the evening comes, and the busy world is hushed, and the fever of life is over and our work is done. Then in thy mercy grant us a safe lodging, and a holy rest, and peace at the last.

> John Henry Cardinal Newman, sermon (1834)

Swami Vivekananda (1863-1902)

His faith emphasized tolerance and accepted all religion as true. That universal truth lies behind all faiths. Everyone possesses a divine spark that can be cultivated through meditation and study. We are all one.

Make me an instrument of Your peace, where there is hatred let me sow love; where there is injury, pardon; where there is doubt, faith; where there is despair, hope; where there is darkness, light; and where there is sadness, joy. Grant that I may not so much seek to be consoled as to console; to be understood as to understand, to be loved as to love. For it is in giving that we receive; it is in pardoning that we are pardoned, and it is in dying that we are born to eternal life.

Saint Francis of Assisi, c. 1181-1226

And He will raise you up on eagles' wings, bear you on the breath of dawn, make you shine like the sun and hold you in His hand.

Hymn sung at the funeral of Helen Hayes,
March 20th, 1993

I am not yet what I would like to be, but this is one thing I do; I keep pressing on.

Saint Paul

Consciousness, a special awareness and sensitivity, permeates all things in the universe—even a rock!

Jacques Barzun

Have we accepted that there is the same divine life in all people, as well as in ourselves? And that this makes a natural and free bond among people?

William Ellery Channing

When we slow down, quiet the mind, and allow ourselves to feel hungry for something that we do not understand, we are dipping into the abundant well of spiritual longing.

Elizabeth Lesser

A founder of the Omega Institute in Rhinebeck, New York, Lesser exhibits remarkable spiritual wisdom with eloquence and conviction.

The Qur'an and the Talmud teach us "He who saves one, saves the world."

Reserving judgment is a matter of infinite hope.

F. Scott Fitzgerald, *The Great Gatsby*

"Hidden causality," the Dalai Lama said, with the Buddha's smile, in support of his belief in the convergence of science and spirituality.

WISDOM

Once inculcated, wisdom can instill gentle strength of understanding; what is true; what is right; what is lasting: wisdom sings a gracious melody of good judgment and good common sense; wisdom introduces us to fairness, love, generosity, beauty, truth and friendship as well…A person blessed with wisdom may be content with a thin wallet and the simplicity of a small cottage, surrounded by colorful, fragrant flowers, within a garden you have cultivated yourself. You are the gardener!

Wisdom can lead us to the deep night fascination of finding a full moon, speckled with white stars and dark moving clouds enlightening the planet. Wisdom speaks to us to be kind and worthy to friends and foes; poor souls and rich braggarts; who may learn from your circle to become wise, so we will become wise. Then we'll have the possibility of discovering our own happiness—the true aim and purpose of life.

Ultimately happiness may outdo wisdom as the goal of those good souls who are pursuing the good life because there's no way you can be completely happy unless you are wise.

Discovering and maintaining the simple moderate life is the most desirable and durable achievement leading us to wisdom.

Small tasks and courtesies reveal the essential truth of life.

The reputation of a thousand years may be determined by the conduct of one hour.
                    Japanese proverb

The greatest of faults is to be conscious of none.
                    Thomas Carlyle

Even greater faults are to continuously offend, knowingly, arrogantly, repeatedly, with no shame whatever.

Every fool will be meddling.
                    Proverbs 20:3

He that wrestles with us strengthens our nerves, and sharpens our skills. Our antagonist is our helper.
                    Edmund Burke

The world is bewildered and is looking for meaning.
                    Mary Sarah Quinn

The reward of suffering is experience.
                    Aeschylus

Is it bad then to be misunderstood? Pythagoras was misunderstood, and Socrates, and Jesus, and Luther, and Copernicus and
Galileo, and Newton and every pure and wise spirit…To be great
is to be misunderstood.

Ralph Waldo Emerson

Gratitude fades.

Tact—the ultimate sensitivity.

The tension between our old "reptilian" brain and our new brain—
metaphor of our own invention—is at the essence of being human. Perhaps this is why we watch with such interest the behavior
of others around us. We realize that in everyone we see ourselves.

Abraham Verghese

In seeing ourselves clearly we are often unnerved.

Only that day dawns to which we are awake. There is more day
to dawn—the sun is but a morning star.

Henry David Thoreau

*Jean-Paul Sartre spoke of the torturous prison experience of
members of the French Resistance. It is not what they do to
you, it is what you do with what they do to you that matters.*

When you're talking you are not learning.

Certain environments, certain modes of life, certain rules of conduct are more conducive to inner and outer harmony than others. There are, in fact, certain roads that one may follow: Simplification of life is one of them.

> Anne Morrow Lindbergh,
> *Gift from the Sea*

Life basically is a matter of winning and retaining your independence.

Genius…means little more than the faculty of perceiving in an unhabitual way.

Be not afraid of life. Believe that life is worth living—and your belief will help create the fact.

> William James

Regret is an emotion we feel when we blame ourselves for unfortunate outcomes that may have been prevented had we only behaved differently in the past…

> Daniel Gilbert

The only thing you know for certain is that you know nothing for certain.

> Alan Jerkens, trainer of Barbaro, the
> celebrated great horse who died a
> tragic death from laminitis disease

Certitude, pushed too far, can be a blindfold.

Certitude is not the test of certainty. What you think you know is not a certainty.

Justice Oliver Wendell Holmes, Jr.

Justice Holmes was a man of extraordinary character and achievement, including a record of personal courage and eloquence.

Delay is always better than error.

Thomas Jefferson

If a nation expects to be ignorant and free…it expects what never was and never will be.

Thomas Jefferson

Freedom and ignorance are incompatible—everywhere.

Quick decisions are unsafe decisions.

Sophocles

Take your time to make crucial choices. Better late than sorry.

Mistakes are the portals of discovery.

James Joyce

If we don't learn something from our mistakes, we are twice bludgeoned.

The wisest mind has something yet to learn.
George Santayana

To live without a sense of promise
To live without a sense of hope
Is not to live at all.

Virtue debases itself in gratifying itself.
Voltaire
Voltaire understood human nature because he was intelligent
enough, and perceptive enough, to see the truth.

Pride goes before destruction, and a haughty spirit before a fall.
Book of Proverbs

When we treat our neighbors as they deserve to be treated, we
make them even worse; when we treat them as if they were who
we wish they were, we improve them.
Johann Wolfgang von Goethe

To carry the spirit of a child into old age.
Aldous Huxley
This is the secret of genius.

Four things come not back: the spoken word; the sped arrow;
time past; the neglected opportunity.
Omar Ibn Al-Halif

People are always blaming their circumstances for what they are. I don't believe in circumstances. The people who get on in this world are the people who get up and look for the circumstances they want, and, if they can't find them, make them.

George Bernard Shaw

Grow up and make your own way.

Politics is supposed to be the second oldest profession. I have come to realize that it bears a very close resemblance to the first.

I was startled to hear, at an unusual hour, the familiar bell of our nearest church, Saint Clothilde. I went to the balcony [in a quiet corner of Paris] and all the household followed me. Through the deep expectant hush we heard, one after another, the bells of Paris calling to each other.

Edith Wharton,
Armistice 1918, November 11th

When seeking advice or help, go to the top.

A key to making a good choice is to recognize the element of excess in the process—too much or too little behavioral activity and thought. Correcting the imbalance is the hard but necessary part of the final decision.

In every enterprise consider where you would come out.

Publius Syrus, 1ˢᵗ century B.C.

Somehow we failed to do so when we chose to invade Iraq.

The manner of giving is worth more than the gift.

Susan Wise Bauer

Nothing contributes so much to tranquilize the mind as steady purpose.

Mary Wollstonecraft Shelley

Definition of the word 'mugwump': a person educated beyond his or her intellect.

Horace Porter

Keep your education and intellect in balance for the good life.

No one can know everything.

Horace

No one should want to. It clogs the mind.

If you would wish another to keep your secret, first keep it yourself.

Seneca

Transcendent wisdom, the delicate fruit of a lifetime of pain.

Joshua Wolf Schenk

Instead of showing ourselves as we truly are, we show ourselves as we believe others want us to be. We wear masks; and with practice we do it better and better, and the masks serve us well— except that it gets very lonely inside the mask, because inside the mask that each of us wears there is a person who both longs to be known, yet fears to be known. Part of what it means to be, is to be you.

> Frederick Buechner

Be yourself.

Think it through rather than think about.

Knowledge comes, but wisdom lingers.

> Alfred, Lord Tennyson

Optimism is a force multiplier.

> General Colin Powell

When April turns to May we have the glory of spring.

Sometimes a confession of ignorance is the only defensible stand.

> Natalie Angier,
> commenting on the nature versus
> nurture debate

Zeitgeist—spirit of the age. (Circling the drain.)

The root of each sin is in a bad thought. We are all only the consequences of what we think.

        Buddha

There is no truth; only truths.

        Albert Camus

The only wisdom we can hope acquire is the wisdom of humility;
humility is endless.

        T. S. Eliot

*Wisdom can be achieved by inner work, through solitary com-
munication with yourself; it also can be achieved when you
communicate with wise persons—such as Leo Tolstoy or
Aristotle.*

Were it not better to forget
Than but remember and regret?

        Letitia Elizabeth Landon

Never does nature say one thing and wisdom another.

        Juvenal

It's never too late to mend.

        English proverb, borrowed from the Greek,
        and current since the sixteenth century

Lord Byron confessed that he loved wisdom more than wisdom loved him.

Don't fight the problem.
>General George Marshall

Intuition is the spark of wisdom within you.

Of the fifty million species on earth, only one has developed a civilization.

Nothing is permanent.

You are what you think. What you think becomes your destiny.

Never be ashamed to admit what you do not know.
>Arabic proverb

The art of being wise is the art of knowing what to overlook.

Whatever you say and however you decide to behave, keep in mind exactly how you would like to see your situation appear on the front page of the *New York Times*.
>Justice John Marshall Harlan, advice to his assistants at the United States Attorney's office

Two people can have a good conversation. Three people cannot.

Waiting for perfection is the greatest enemy of the current good.
          Voltaire

Envy kills itself with its own cudgel.

An unlearned carpenter once said in my hearing: "There is very little difference between one man and another, but what little there is, is very important." This distinction seems to me to go to the root of the matter.
          William James

I assert that nothing ever comes to pass without a cause.
          Reverend Jonathan Edwards, Connecticut
          fiery preacher who is said to have blistered
          the pews (1703-1758)

Destiny is not a matter of chance. It is a matter of choice.
          George H. W. Bush

Treat your friend as if he or she will one day be your enemy, and your enemy as if he or she will one day be your friend.
          Laberius (105-43 B.C.)

Without memory wisdom hides.

There is a sadness of heart that goes along with much joy.
Justice Oliver Wendell Holmes, Jr.

What cowardice it is to be dismayed by the happiness of others and devastated by their good fortune.
Charles de Secondat, baron de Montesquieu

Civility costs nothing.
English proverb (not recorded before the nineteenth century)

In place of fundamental truths I put fundamental possibilities— provisionally assured guides by which one lives and thinks.
Friedrich Nietzsche

Better to remain silent and be thought a fool than to speak out and remove all doubt.
Abraham Lincoln

Grownups never understand anything for themselves, and it is tiresome for children to be always and forever explaining things to them.
Antoine de Saint-Exupéry

At our fiftieth reunion at Yale I chose to quote a Sanskrit Hindu mantra to salute the great durable Class of 1944: "Participate with joy in the sorrows of the world."

Sweeping generalizations skid over truth.

The most manifest sign of wisdom is a continual cheerfulness: This state is like that of things in the regions above the moon, always clean and serene.

> Michel de Montaigne

In wine is truth.

> Plato

Be lamps unto yourself.

> Buddha

Embracing an error simply continues the mistake.

When you have nothing to say, say nothing.

> Charles Caleb Colton

Absence of evidence is not evidence of absence.

> Carl Sagan

A person who knows little likes to talk, and one who knows much mostly keeps silent.

> Jean-Jacques Rousseau

I've taken my fun where I've found it.

> Rudyard Kipling

Intellectual passion drives out sensuality.
> Leonardo da Vinci

No, sensuality drives out intellectual passion.

All negative thoughts have negative results.
> Alexandra Stoddard

Some people get it and some people never get it.
> Bishop John Bowen Coburn

Do you wish people to think well of you? Don't speak well of yourself.
> Blaise Pascal

How sharp the point of this remembrance is!
> William Shakespeare

Bring out the best of what is in you.
> Alexandra Stoddard

Any man who does not believe in miracles is not a realist.
> David Ben-Gurion

Whatever I am offered in devotion, with a pure heart—a leaf, a flower, a fruit or water—I accept with joy.
> Bhagavad-Gita

Once a wise man was asked, "What is intelligence?" He answered, "Modesty." Then he was asked, "What is modesty?" And he answered, "Intelligence."

Solomon ben Judah ibn Gabirol

Intelligence does not equal wisdom. Wisdom is profound, while intelligence alone can be superficial.

No one can interpret a prophecy except after the event.

Nikos Kasantzakis

We forge gradually our greatest instrument for understanding the world—introspection. We discover that humanity may resemble us very considerably—that the best way of knowing the inwardness of our neighbors is to know ourselves.

Walter Lippman

Sublimity is the echo of a noble mind.

Longinus, 1st century A.D.

Affliction is the good man's shining time.

Abigail Adams, quoting the English poet
Edward Young on successful moments of the
American Revolution, 1776

"Pride goes before a fall" was my mother's favorite warning to her unruly children.

A good mind possesses a kingdom.

Seneca

If we had no faults, we should not take so much pleasure in noting those of others.

La Rochefoucauld

Tact is after all a kind of mind-reading.

Sarah Orne Jewett

Everything and everyone is connected.

The spirit of the tea ceremony—harmony, reverence, purity, and tranquility—matches perfectly the spirit of Zen.

Toichi Yoshioka

I take it to be the highest instance of a noble mind to bear great qualities without discovering in a man's behavior any consciousness that he is superior to the rest of the world.

Richard Steele

Noble minds rise without expressing superiority.

If experience is the key of wisdom, truth and beauty are our goal in life.

It is of immense importance to learn to laugh at ourselves.

Katherine Mansfield

True wisdom lies in gathering the precious things out of each day as it goes by.

E. S. Bouton

The more a person analyzes his inner self, the more signifi-cant he seems to himself. This is the first lesson of wisdom— let us be humble, and we will become wise. Let us know our weakness, and it will give us power.

To live content with small means, to seek elegance rather than luxury, and refinement rather than fashion, to be worthy, not respectable, and wealthy, not rich, to study hard, think quietly, talk gently, act frankly, to listen to stars and birds, to babes and sages, with open heart, to bear all cheerfully, do all bravely, await occasions, hurry never. In a word, to let the spiritual, unbidden and unconscious, grow up through the common. This is to be my symphony.

William Ellery Channing

CONCLUSION

A Note to My Reader

Today at noon on April 14th, 2009, I am somewhat saddened to find myself writing down this final page of my manuscript, *Figure It Out*, that I began with some humility and trepidation over half a century ago—committing myself to collecting, analyzing, and printing out a book of gems of wisdom I have enjoyed enormously putting together in twenty-seven categories from Love to Wisdom, with a most thoughtful and kind foreword by my beloved wife Alexandra, my partner and companion during most of these years. Alexandra has made it possible for me to finish up this work of collection and research—truly a lifetime of personal satisfaction. I am most grateful to her for the care and love that has led to this day of conclusion. Now I intend to share these gems that have meant so much to me with you, my reader, in hopes we together can also share this wisdom with our children, grandchildren, and great grandchildren to come . . .

With great affection and love,
Peter

Authors & Sources Index

SUBJECT INDEX

ability:

    Class can be defined as the ability in any situation to be yourself, 189

    It is a great ability to be able to conceal one's ability, 188

absence:

    Absence of evidence is not evidence of absence, 230

action:

    Action that does not lead to reflection is more gravely incomplete, 187

    I have only a second-rate brain but I think I have a capacity for action, 190

    Thought which does not ultimately guide action is incomplete, 187

Adam, 81

advantage:

    let not advantage slip, 65

adversity:

    Prosperity makes friends, adversity tries them, 203

the *Aeneid*, 150

Aesop's Fly, 106

affliction:

Affliction is the good man's shining time, 59, 232

age, 163–167

The essence of age is intellect, 165

He who is calm and of a happy nature will hardly feel the pressure of age, 166

See also **old age**

air:

a blessing in the air, 18

America:

America is great because she is good and if America ever ceases to be good, America will cease to be great, 148

America is more capable of enthusiasm, 24

In America the law is King, 36

Americans:

Americans like things quick, easy, and cheap, iii

antagonist:

Our antagonist is our helper, 218

arena:

The credit belongs to the man who is actually in the arena, 184

arguing:

Be calm in arguing, 160

arrow:

Four things come not back: … the sped arrow, 222

art, 191–195

Art is the transforming experience, 193

Art is unthinkable without risk and spiritual self-sacrifice, 193

Conversation … is the art of never being a bore, 205

Criticism is easy, art is difficult, 192

The future of art is in light, 193

A work of art is never finished, only abandoned, 192

common sense:
Common sense is not so common, 156
competence:
higher qualities than competence. The rarest and highest is honor, 170
competition:
The healthiest competition occurs when average people put in above-average effort, 132
compliment:
A compliment is the only thing you pay that costs nothing, 179
concentration:
Concentration is everything, 130
confession:
Sometimes a confession of ignorance is the only defensible stand, 225
conscious:
The greatest of faults is to be conscious of none, 219
consciousness:
Consciousness … permeates all things in the universe—even a rock, 214
The cosmos and human consciousness are infinite, 212
console:
Grant that I may not so much seek to be consoled as to console, 214
conversation:
Conversation … is the art of never being a bore, 205
corner:
Start somewhere in a corner and go from there, 156
correct:
How much easier it is to be critical than to be correct, 97

difference:

little difference between one man and another … is very
important, 228

difficult:

Criticism is easy, art is difficult, 192

There is no large and difficult task than can't be divided into
little, easy tasks, 133

dignity:

Leisure with dignity, 96

discontent:

What good is discontent?, 157

discovery:

Mistakes are the portals of discovery, 221

divine:

there is the same divine life in all people, 214

do:

It is not so important what we say, it is important what we do,
188

To know how to do something well is to enjoy it, 190

this is one thing I do; I keep pressing on, 214

done:

Well done is better than well said, 185

doubt:

Better to remain silent and be thought a fool than to speak out
and remove all doubt, 229

drama:

Drama demands resolution, 87

dream:

I have a dream, 183

dust:

What a dust I do raise, 106

evolution:

Evolution is a sequence of accidents, 140

excellence:

Chase perfection, and settle for excellence along the way, 159

The secret of joy in work is contained in one word: *excellence,* 190

executive:

The best executive, 131

expected:

What we least expected generally happens, 118

To whom much is given, much is expected, 211

experience:

Art is the transforming experience, 193

To be told is not equal to the experience, 113

Experience is helpful, but it is judgment that matters, 146

No man's knowledge can go beyond his experience, 97

The reward of suffering is experience, 218

self-awareness makes human experience resonant, 159

experiments:

I love fools' experiments, I am always making them, 133

expert:

An expert is one who knows more and more about less and less, 136

exploring:

the end of all our exploring, 60

exuberance:

Exuberance increases risk-taking, innovative thinking and the anticipation of success, 136

eye:

Monet is but an eye … but good God, what an eye!, 195

failure:

Success is going from failure to failure without loss of enthusiasm, 135

guest:
After three days men grow weary, of a wench, a guest, and rainy weather, 207

happiest:
    The happiest man is, 22
happiness, 21–26
    beauty that come from happiness, enthusiasm, success, 22
    genuine human happiness, 22
    guardians and inheritors of happiness, 22
    happiness more luminous and intense, 50
    Noble people rejoice in the happiness and success of others, 133
    Pleasure is only the shadow of Happiness, 182
    reward of happiness, 25
    Seeking happiness outside of ourselves, 25
    That is happiness, 22
    What cowardice it is to be dismayed by the happiness of others, 229
happy:
    Happy families are all alike, 24
    Man's real life is happy, chiefly, because he is ever expecting that it will be soon be so, 103
    only ones among you who will be really happy, 25
    way to be happy, 24
harmony:
    inner and outer harmony, 220
hatred:
    Hatred is the winter of the heart, 56
health:
    gap in wealth and health … is the greatest single problem and danger facing the world, 180

Give me health and a day, and I will make the pomp of
emperors ridiculous, 156
Health is the first muse and sleep is the condition to produce
it, 156
Virtue is a kind of health, 55

hearts:

stout hearts and sharp words, 78

helper:

Our antagonist is our helper, 218

hero:

A hero does not die, 101
A hero is no braver than an ordinary man, 101
no man is a hero to his valet, 102

heroes, 99–102

heroism:

Each of us has some capacity for heroism, 101

hill:

we shall be a city set upon a hill, 149

history, 139–152

History is the essence of innumerable biographies, 148
I like the dreams for the future better than the history of the
past, 117

honest:

He who says there is no such thing as an honest man, you
may be sure is himself a knave, 170

honesty:

All writers … have a kind of "terrible honesty," 80
Define wisdom as the application of truth and honesty to
everyday life, 172
It takes a great deal of honesty to produce a little literature, 86

honey:

The Pedigree of Honey, 131

leaders:

Wise leaders don't think abstractly, 86

learn:

first thing you learn in marriage, 60

I am always ready to learn, although I do not always like being taught, 201

I never learn anything talking, 94

It is of immense importance to learn to laugh at ourselves, 233

learn as if you will live forever, 43

Learn to die, 43–44

We can learn even from our enemies, 95

The wisest mind has something yet to learn, 222

leisure:

Leisure with dignity, 96

letter:

A letter lights up the whole room, 80

letters:

Letters . . . are the fossils of feeling, 87

liberal arts:

Faithful study of the liberal arts humanizes character and permits it not be cruel, 201

liberty:

spirit of liberty, 42

library:

Here is his library, but his study is out of doors, 199

lie:

a half truth is a whole lie, 31

Judges lie, 31

life, 103–119

The Aim, reached or not, makes great the life, 116

personality:

The imprints of childhood are the strongest and most enduring stamp of personality, 187

Peter Rabbit, 71

philosopher:

To be a philosopher, 91

philosophy, 89–97

nowadays there are philosophy professors, but no philosophers, 90

Philosophy … is our more or less dumb sense of what life honestly and deeply means, 89

play:

Celebration is yet another form of human play, 154

Intellectual play … is serious business, 112

Play one's part and contribute to the whole effort, 144

pleasure:

If we had no faults, we should not take so much pleasure in noting those of others, 233

Pleasure is only the shadow of Happiness, 182

Pleasure is the beginning and the end, 25

There is no such thing as pure pleasure, 108

plot:

The great primordial plot, 51

poetry:

Poetry begins in emotion recollected in tranquility, 78

Poetry occurs when, 79

politics:

In war you can only be killed once, but in politics many times, 150

popularity:

Popularity? It is glory's small change, 190

Breinigsville, PA USA
03 June 2010
239161BV00003B/4/P

9 781616 190378